Gospel Light's

Fruitful Lives

Kids' Sermons and Object Talks

Based on the fruit of the Spirit

Gospel Light

HOW TO MAKE CLEAN COPIES FROM THIS BOOK

You may make copies of portions of this book with a clean conscience if

- you (or someone in your organization) are the original purchaser;
- you are using the copies you make for a noncommercial purpose (such as teaching or promoting your ministry) within your church or organization;
- you follow the instructions provided in this book.

However, it is ILLEGAL for you to make copies if

- you are using the material to promote, advertise or sell a product or service other than for ministry fund-raising;
- you are using the material in or on a product for sale; or
- you or your organization are not the original purchaser of this book.

By following these guidelines you help us keep our products affordable.
Thank you,
Gospel Light

Gospel Light

Editorial Staff

Publisher, William T. Greig
Senior Consulting Publisher, Dr. Elmer L. Towns
Publisher, Research, Planning and Development, Billie Baptiste
Managing Editor, Lynnette Pennings, M.A.
Senior Consulting Editor, Wesley Haystead, M.S.Ed
Senior Editor, Biblical and Theological Issues, Bayard Taylor, M.Div.
Senior Advisor, Biblical and Theological Issues, Dr. Gary S. Greig
Senior Editor, Sheryl Haystead
Editorial Team, Amanda Abbas, Debbie Barber, Mary Gross, Karen McGraw
Designer, Zelle Olson

Scripture quotations are taken from the *Holy Bible, New International Version®*. Copyright © 1973, 1978, 1984 by International Bible Society. Used by permission of Zondervan Publishing House. All rights reserved.

© 2001 Gospel Light, Ventura, CA 93006. All rights reserved. Printed in the U.S.A.

Contents

Fruitful Lives Kids' Sermons and Object Talks

Kid Sermon and Object Talk

TIPS

The fruitful lives object talks can draw children in and help them understand how the fruit of God's Spirit has been shown in the lives of Christians throughout history. These object talks can be used as children's sermons or used to supplement any Sunday School curriculum. They can also be used to augment any children's ministry program, day school or homeschool curriculum.

Getting the Most Out of a Kid Sermon and Object Talk

• Preparation is the key to object talks! Read an object talk at least several days ahead of time to give ample time to gather the needed materials and to find out more about the person in question, as your interest dictates.

• If you are interested in learning more about the person whose life is featured, try the *Dictionary of American Biography*, the Internet or an encyclopedia for more information. Download or photocopy photos of the person for your students to see. Libraries may also have biographies available.

• Whenever possible, invite students to participate in the object talk. Ask a different student each week to read the Bible verse aloud (highlight the verse in your Bible and mark its location with a bookmark).

• Occasionally describe situations in which learning about the person about whom you're telling or in which understanding the lesson focus has helped you. Tell students how the Bible verse has been important to you.

• Because of the limited space available in each talk for the study of the lives of various well-known Christians, set up an information station where students may learn more about each featured individual. Pictures, books, printouts of information gleaned from the Internet and objects related to the time period of that person's life can all enhance a student's understanding of what God did through that person's life.

Using a Kid Sermon and Object Talk During Adult Worship

If the children in your church are in the adult service during the first part of the service, consider using the object talk as the basis for a weekly children's sermon. Introduce the idea of the object talks to the adult audience by saying, **This year our children are learning all about the fruits of the Spirit. Today they will be studying _____.** Give the talk and then, if possible, ask one or more of the Discussion Questions found in bold print at the end of each talk.

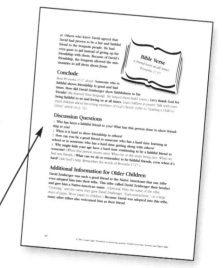

Helping Kids Make the Transition to Adult Worship

For a few moments, let's do a little pretending. Let's pretend that we are six-year-old children and that we are sitting in the adult worship service of our church. What words will we hear that we don't understand? What books are we asked to use that we don't know how to read? What happens in front that we can't see because we are small? What are we expected to do that is confusing to us? How long do we have to sit still when we are not used to sitting?

As you think through some of the things your children experience in a typical worship service, you may come to the realization that the adult worship service sometimes becomes an uncomfortable, passive experience for a child rather than an opportunity to praise and worship God.

However, you as a children's program leader, as well as parents, pastor and others involved in leading the adult worship service, CAN take many specific actions to make the service more meaningful and enjoyable for children. Whether the children in your church are approaching the first time they will attend the service, attend the service only occasionally, frequently attend at least part of the service or are about to be promoted from their own children's church program into regular attendance at the adult worship service, here are some specific suggestions to help them enjoy and benefit from being with the grown-ups in "Big Church."

When Children Are in the Worship Service

Encourage parents to sit with their children near the front of the worship service. They will not only see and hear better, but they will also have more of a sense that the person up front is speaking to them. Proximity encourages participation.

Arrange for those who are involved in leading worship to meet periodically with the children in fairly small groups. This can be done briefly at the end of Sunday School or as a part of another children's program. Use this time to explain one feature of the service the children are about to attend. If this is done every week or on some other regularly scheduled basis, the children can gradually be introduced to the entire spectrum of worship activities that occur in your services.

A significant bonus of this approach is that children will also get to know your leaders as friends who care about them, rather than viewing them as strangers who lead unfamiliar ceremonies at a distance. Perhaps of even greater significance, this brief time of interaction will alert these leaders to the presence of children in the worship service, helping the leaders become more effective in including children in the worship experiences.

HINT: If you invite someone to meet with the children and this person is not experienced in speaking at a child's level, structure the time as an interview which one of the children's teachers or leaders will conduct. Let your invited guest know ahead of time the specific questions that will be asked.

Provide parents with a sheet of tips of things to have the child do before, during and after the service in order to gain maximum understanding and participation.

Tips for Parents

Before the Service:

• Sit near the front where your child can easily see what is happening.

• If your church prints an order of service in the bulletin, help your child identify, find and mark locations of hymns and Scripture readings.

• Let your child underline all the words in the bulletin he or she can read.

• Briefly explain the meaning of any difficult words or phrases in at least the first hymn you will sing.

• Share your own feelings about the hymns or songs to be sung: "This is one of my favorites," "I really like to sing this because it helps me tell God I love Him," "This is one I've never learned—I hope it's easy to sing," etc.

During the Service:

• Let your child help hold the hymnal or song sheet. Run your finger beneath the words being sung to help your child follow along. If your church displays the words of each song on an overhead, make sure you sit where your child can see the words.

• Touch your child (not just when the wiggles are in action) to build a sense of warmth in being together.

• Provide writing and/or drawing materials. Encourage your child to write or draw about things he or she sees or hears during the service. ("Draw a picture of something the pastor talks about in his sermon.")

• If there is a time of greeting one another, introduce your child to those around you.

• Let your child take part in passing the offering plate, registration cards or other items distributed throughout the congregation.

After the Service:

• Express your appreciation at being in church with the child.

• Commend your child for specific times when he or she was participating well. ("You really did a good job singing that first hymn.")

• Talk about what went on in the service. Avoid making this sound like an exam, but ask one or two questions to let the child know that you expect him or her to be listening. A few good questions to use are "What is one thing you remember from the service?" "Which song did you like best?" "What Bible person did the pastor talk about?" and "What was the pastor trying to teach us about?"

• Share your own answers to those questions, or let your child ask you any questions he or she desires.

• Explain one or two things that happened in the service that you think your child was interested in or could have been confused by.

Tips for the Children's Program Leader

As the children's program leader, you can also take specific actions to make the adult worship service more meaningful to the child. Look at everything that is done through a "six-year-old's filter." Ask yourself, *What would a child understand from what we just did?* This is not a plea to conduct six-year-old-level worship services, but it will help adults become aware of children's presence and their right to be led in meaningful worship of the Lord. The child will not understand EVERYTHING that occurs in every service, but the child deserves to understand SOMETHING in every service.

Meet with the person(s) responsible for planning the worship service and talk about ways to make the service more helpful to children. Consider these ideas:

• Choose at least one hymn or song with a repeating chorus, which makes it easier for children to learn and participate.

• Choose at least one hymn or song with fairly simple words and melody.

• Introduce at least some hymns with a brief explanation for children.

• Once or twice in the service mention, "Our children are worshiping with us and we want to help them know what we are singing (talking) about." This will help raise the congregation's awareness of their responsibility to guide children and will also explain some things to adults and teenagers that they might be embarrassed to ask about.

• Provide simple explanations of special observances (baptism, the Lord's Supper, etc.).

• When inviting people to greet one another, remind them to include children in their interaction. Instructions such as "Talk to at least one person from a generation other than your own" or "Greet someone who is now attending school" are enjoyable ways to alert adults without making the children feel put on the spot.

• Find ways to involve children in some specific aspects of the service. Many churches are familiar with occasionally having a children's choir sing, but often the children feel more like outside performers than participants in family worship. Occasionally invite children to assist in receiving the offering (perhaps have parent-child teams), handing out bulletins, reading Scripture, answering a question, etc. Some churches periodically give their choir the day off and form a family choir with moms, dads and kids singing a simple song with other families after a brief rehearsal or two.

• If the adults in your congregation wear name tags, provide name tags for the children, too.

• Provide clipboards, paper and crayons for children to use during the service. Before the sermon, the person leading the service can suggest that the children listen for a particular person or event during the sermon and draw a picture about that person or event on the paper. Children may pick up the clipboards during a hymn or some other appropriate time just before the sermon.

• Make a checklist of things for the children to listen for during the service. As the children hear one of the things listed, they check it off the list.

• Several months before children are promoted from their children's church program into regular attendance at the adult worship service, plan to have the children participate in a portion of each service each week or the entire service once a month.

• Ask a person with video equipment to make a recording of the entire worship service. Then, occasionally choose specific parts of the service to show and explain.

• If the order of worship is printed in your bulletin, give each child a bulletin and briefly explain the order of worship. Describe in childlike terms how each part of the service helps us worship God.

• If your congregation sings a song often (such as the "Doxology" or "Gloria Patri"), teach it to the children. You may also help them become familiar with the Lord's Prayer or the Apostles' Creed (if they are used in your church) by repeating them from time to time in your program.

• Help children understand that worship is anything we do that shows that we love and respect God. Use your conversation to help your children understand how praise, music, prayer and learning from God's Word are all important aspects of worship.

Leading a Child to Christ

One of the greatest privileges of serving in children's programs is to help children become members of God's family. Some children, especially those from Christian homes, may be ready to believe in Jesus Christ as their Savior earlier than others. Ask God to prepare the children to receive the good news about Jesus and prepare you to communicate effectively with them.

Talk individually with children. Something as important as a child's personal relationship with Jesus Christ can be handled more effectively one-on-one than in a group. A child needs to respond individually to the call of God's love. This response needs to be a genuine response to God—not because the child wants to please peers, parents or you, the leader.

Follow these basic steps in talking simply with children about how to become members of God's family. The evangelism booklet *God Loves You!* (available from Gospel Light) is an effective guide to follow. Show the child what God says in His Word. Ask the questions suggested to encourage thinking and comprehending.

1. God wants you to become His child. (See John 1:12.) **Do you know why God wants you in His family?** (See 1 John 4:8.)

2. You and all the people in the world have done wrong things. (See Romans 3:23.) **The Bible word for doing wrong is sin. What do you think should happen to us when we sin?** (See Romans 6:23.)

3. God loves you so much He sent His Son to die on the cross for your sins. Because Jesus never sinned, He is the only One who can take the punishment for your sins. (See 1 Corinthians 15:3; 1 John 4:14.) **The Bible tells us that God raised Jesus from the dead and that He is alive forever.**

4. Are you sorry for your sins? Do you believe Jesus died to be your Savior? If you do believe and you are sorry for your sins, God forgives all your sins. (See 1 John 1:9.)

When you talk to God, tell Him that you believe He gave His Son, Jesus Christ, to take your punishment. Also tell God you are sorry for your sins. Tell Him that He is a great and wonderful God. It is easy to talk to God. He is ready to listen. What you are going to tell Him is something He has been waiting to hear.

5. The Bible says that when you believe in Jesus, God's Son, you receive God's gift of eternal life. This gift makes you a child of God. This means God is with you now and forever. (See John 3:16.)

Give your pastor the names of those who make decisions to become members of God's family. Encourage the child to tell his or her family about the decision. Children who make decisions need follow-up to help them grow in Christ.

NOTE: The Bible uses many terms and images to express the concept of salvation. Children often do not understand or may develop misconceptions about these terms, especially terms that are highly symbolic. (Remember the trouble Nicodemus, a respected teacher, had in trying to understand the meaning of being "born again"?) Many people talk with children about "asking Jesus into your heart." The literal-minded child is likely to develop strange ideas from the imagery of those words. The idea of being a child of God (see John 1:12) is perhaps the simplest portrayal the New Testament provides.

God's Word in English

Patiently keep doing what God wants you to do.

Teacher's Materials

Bible with bookmark at 1 Kings 8:61, several different versions of the Bible and/or several written in different languages.

Introduce the Object Talk

God wants us to keep showing our love of and obedience to Him. Let's find out about one man who had to patiently keep doing what God wanted him to do.

Bible Verse

Your hearts must be fully committed to the Lord our God, to live by his decrees and obey his commands. 1 Kings 8:61

Present the Object Talk

1. Invite volunteers to examine the Bibles you collected. **In what ways are these books alike? How are they different?** Children respond. **Today the Bible has been written in many different languages so that people all over the world can read God's Word. But a long time ago in the**

1500s, the Bible was only written in Latin. Because only a few people could understand Latin, most people couldn't read God's Word for themselves.

2. One man named William Tyndale, however, wanted people to have Bibles they could read. William was a teacher who lived in England. But the leaders in England didn't want people to be able to read the Bible for themselves! William didn't let that stop him. He understood Latin, so he carefully translated the New Testament into English. Soon people all over England were buying and reading this English New Testament.

The leaders, however, were so angry they bought all the English New Testaments they could find and burned them! William was very discouraged. But then he heard some good news. The money William had earned from selling the English New Testaments to the angry leaders was enough to print even more New Testaments than before! William Tyndale patiently worked to print the English New

Testaments over again so that people once again could read God's Word!

Conclude

Read 1 Kings 8:61 aloud. **When we are "committed to the Lord," it means we patiently keep doing what's right, even when it's hard. What did William Tyndale do, even though it was hard?** (He translated the New Testament into English. He sold copies of the New Testament so that he could print more.) **God promises to help us.** Lead children in prayer, asking God to help children patiently continue to obey Him.

Bible Verse
Your hearts must be fully committed to the Lord our God, to live by his decrees and obey his commands. 1 Kings 8:61

Discussion Questions

1. What do you think it means to commit our hearts to God? (To love God more than anyone or anything.) **How will this help us to do the right thing?** (When we are committed to God, we want to please Him in everything we do.)

2. What are some of the things we know God wants us to do? (Show love to others. Speak kind words to others. Tell the truth. Pray to Him.) **When would kids your age need patience to keep doing those good things?** (When they don't feel like being kind. When people aren't being kind to them. When people make fun of them.)

3. What is another word for doing what God wants you to do? ("Obeying.") **When is a time it might be hard to patiently keep obeying God?** (When friends ask you to do something you know is wrong, or they don't care if you do the right thing or not.)

4. What are some things you can do to keep doing what God wants you to do? (Pray to God for His help. Talk with others who love God.)

Additional Information for Older Children

William Tyndale's first New Testament was printed in 1526. About 10 years later, William was killed because he translated the Bible. Then within five years of his death, the king of England approved another English Bible (based on William's translation) and required every church to make copies available to the people!

Songs of Joy

God's gifts to us bring joy and cause our thankfulness to overflow.

Teacher's Materials
Bible with bookmark at Psalm 28:7, hymnal.

Introduce the Object Talk
Remembering God's gifts to us helps us be joyful and want to thank God. Let's look at a book written by people whose thankfulness to God couldn't help but show.

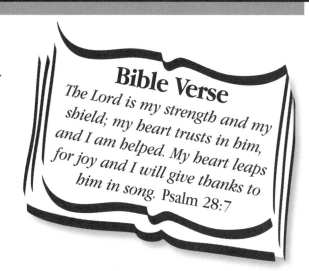

Bible Verse
The Lord is my strength and my shield; my heart trusts in him, and I am helped. My heart leaps for joy and I will give thanks to him in song. Psalm 28:7

Present the Object Talk
1. Open hymnal and show it to children. **What is in this book? How are books like this used?** Volunteers respond. **Hymnals are books of songs about God. These songs were written by many different people who loved God and wanted others to love Him, too. One hymn writer's name was Francis Crosby. (She is often called by the nickname "Fanny.")**

2. Francis Crosby was born in New York in 1820. When Francis was only six weeks old, she became sick and eventually became blind. Then shortly after Francis became blind, her father died and her family became very poor.

In spite of the bad things that happened to her, Francis Crosby didn't feel sorry for herself. When she grew up, Francis became a teacher at a school for the blind. She also was a concert singer and played the piano and the harp. And Francis wrote songs, thousands of them! During her lifetime, Francis Crosby wrote over 8,000 songs and poems—and many of them were written to show her love and thankfulness to God.

Conclude

Read Psalm 28:7 aloud. **Among the good gifts God gave Francis Crosby were some special talents. What were some of her talents?** (Francis could play the piano and harp. She could sing well and write songs. She was a teacher.) **How did Francis use her gifts to show her thanks to God?** (She wrote and sang songs about God. She taught others about God.) Lead children in prayer, thanking God for His gifts to them.

Bible Verse

The Lord is my strength and my shield; my heart trusts in him, and I am helped. My heart leaps for joy and I will give thanks to him in song. Psalm 28:7

Discussion Questions

1. What are some of the good gifts God gives us? (People who love us. Food. Clothing. Forgiveness of sins. Talents.)

2. What can you do to thank God for these gifts? (Tell Him words of praise and thanks. Tell other people how great He is. Sing songs of thankfulness to Him. Use the gifts to praise Him.)

3. The best gift God ever gave us was His Son, Jesus. Jesus makes it possible for us to become members of God's family. What are some ways to show we are thankful for Jesus? (Say prayers of thanks to God. Sing songs about Jesus.) Talk with interested children about becoming members of God's family (refer to "Leading a Child to Christ" article on p. 12).

Additional Information for Older Children

In a church hymnal, use bookmarks or Post-it Notes to mark several hymns written by Francis Crosby. Her hymns include "To God Be the Glory," "Blessed Assurance," "I Am Thine O Lord," "Praise Him! Praise Him!" and "Redeemed." Volunteers find and read or sing hymns written by Francis Crosby. **What do these hymns talk about? What did Francis Crosby want to thank God for? What words or phrases remind you of being happy or joyful?**

Home Security

When we trust in God's care, His peace helps us not to worry.

Teacher's Materials
Bible with bookmark at Psalm 29:11, one or more items people use for home security (warning sign, lock, keys, light, etc.).

Introduce the Object Talk
When we trust in God's care, the peace He gives us will help us not to worry. Let's find out how some people trusted in God and how God helped them in a very scary situation.

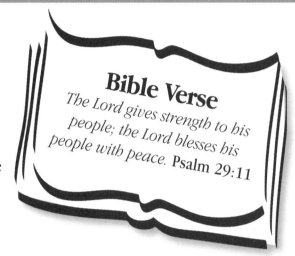

Bible Verse
The Lord gives strength to his people; the Lord blesses his people with peace. Psalm 29:11

Present the Object Talk
1. Show items you brought. **What do people use these items for? What are some other things people depend on to protect them?** Children respond. **Two missionaries, John Paton and his wife, knew one night that they needed protection.**

2. John Paton and his wife were missionaries on Tanna, an island near the country of Australia in the late 1800s. One tribe didn't like the missionaries and wanted to kill them. Late one night the Patons realized that angry warriors from this tribe had surrounded their home. All night long the Patons prayed to God. In the morning the warriors were gone! The Patons thanked God for keeping them safe.

About a year later, the tribal chief who had planned the attack became a Christian. The chief asked John who the men were the chief had seen guarding the missionary home the night of the attack. John told the chief that he and his wife were the only people there. Both men then realized that the warriors had seen angels God sent to protect the missionaries.

Conclude

Read Psalm 29:11 aloud. **What does this verse say that God does? What does it mean to say we have God's peace?** (We can feel safe because we know God always cares for us.) **How did the Patons show that they believed this about God?** Children respond. Lead children in prayer.

Bible Verse

The Lord gives strength to his people; the Lord blesses his people with peace. Psalm 29:11

Discussion Questions

1. **What are some scary situations kids your age often face? What do you know about God that might help someone in a situation like this to have peace?**

2. **What are some ways God has cared for you or for someone you know?** Describe one or more ways God has cared for you before asking children to respond.

3. **How can you remember to trust God's care when you are worried or afraid?** (Pray. Read a Bible verse. Talk to someone who loves God.)

Additional Information for Older Children

When John Paton became a missionary, one of the first things he had to do was learn the language of the people on the island of Tanna. Their language, Tannese, had never been written down! But John thought of a way to write down the words. He was even able to print the Bible for the people of Tanna. John later wrote the story of his life in a book titled *John G. Paton, Missionary to the Cannibals.*

House Afire

Teacher's Materials

Bible with bookmark at Psalm 33:20, an item from your home you would want to save in the event of a house fire; optional—copy of "Upon the Burning of Our House" by Anne Bradstreet (available on the Internet and in most American literature anthologies).

Bible Verse
We wait in hope for the Lord; he is our help and our shield.
Psalm 33:20

Introduce the Object Talk

Because we know that God will always keep His promises, we can be patient and depend on Him. Let's find out how one person showed hope and trust in God's promises.

Present the Object Talk

1. What would you try to save if your house caught on fire? Volunteers respond. Show item that you brought. **This is something I would not want to lose in a fire.** Explain why the item is important to you. **A woman named Anne Bradstreet realized that something else was important when her house burned down.**

2. Anne Bradstreet, her husband and her parents sailed on a boat from England to America in 1630. They began living in the Massachusetts Bay Colony. One night, Anne woke up to the sounds of a fire. Anne and her family escaped the blaze, but they couldn't save anything at all in their house. The entire house and everything in it were destroyed!

Anne wrote a poem about her feelings when her home burned. In the poem, Anne said that she would miss the many things that were destroyed, but the things most important to her—God's promises—could not be burned. Anne believed that God's promises were her most important treasures. Through her poem, Anne showed

that she trusted God to care for her family and that she chose to hope and trust in God's promises. (Optional: Read "Upon the Burning of Our House" aloud.)

Bible Verse

We wait in hope for the Lord; he is our help and our shield.

Psalm 33:20

Conclude

Read Psalm 33:20 aloud. **How did Anne Bradstreet show hope in God? Why do you think Anne chose to respond the way she did?** Children respond. **Let's ask God to help us remember to depend on His promises and be patient.** Lead children in prayer.

Discussion Questions

1. **What are some promises you know God has made? What do you know about God that would make you trust Him to keep His promises?**

2. **What might help us wait patiently for God to keep His promises?** (Remembering the times He has helped us in the past. Thanking Him for His love for us. Praying and asking Him for patience.)

3. **What are some of God's promises for which we never have to wait?** (God's promise to always be with us. God's promise to give us courage.)

Additional Information for Older Children

During the time when Anne Bradstreet lived, few women could read or write, let alone write poems! But when she was growing up, Anne's father had worked for an important man in England. Because her father had such an important job, he was able to pay people to teach Anne how to play music and how to speak and write several languages. Later on, after she had moved to America, Anne used her talent for writing to describe her love for her husband, her children and, most of all, her love for God.

Joy in the Pit

Joyfully celebrate God's help and protection.

Teacher's Materials
Bible with bookmark at Psalm 92:4; shovel.

Introduce the Object Talk
We can joyfully celebrate God's help and protection! Let's find out about a man who celebrated God at every opportunity he had!

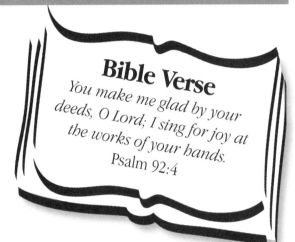

Bible Verse
You make me glad by your deeds, O Lord; I sing for joy at the works of your hands.
Psalm 92:4

Present the Object Talk

1. Ask a volunteer to demonstrate how to use a shovel. **What are some hard jobs people have to do with shovels?** (Dig ditches. Dig in fields. Dig big holes.) **A man named George Chen had to dig with a shovel every day for more than five years doing a job no one else wanted!**

2. George Chen lived in China and was sent to prison because he was a Christian and came from a wealthy family. In that prison, no one was allowed to talk about God, read a Bible or pray.

Each person in the prison had a job to do. George's job was to shovel out the huge hole in the ground where all of the waste from the prison was put. Each day the guards lowered George and his shovel into the pit. All day long George worked hard.

Most people would have hated such a smelly, dirty job! But George soon discovered that because the pit was so dirty and smelly, no guards came to check on him while he worked. Every day George was free to sing songs of praise to God, to pray out loud and to recite Bible verses he had memorized. If he had worked inside the prison in a cleaner place, he would not have been able to sing and pray aloud! George joyfully thanked God—even when it was hard!

Conclude

Read Psalm 92:4 aloud. **When was George Chen able to sing to God and praise Him? We don't have to wait to be alone or in a smelly pit to sing and praise God! We can praise Him anytime!** Lead children in prayer, praising God for specific actions He has done (created the world, forgiven our sins, answered our prayers).

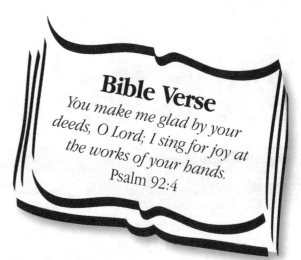

Bible Verse
You make me glad by your deeds, O Lord; I sing for joy at the works of your hands.
Psalm 92:4

Discussion Questions

1. When has God helped or protected you or someone you know? Share an age-appropriate example of your own before asking children to answer.

2. When are some times a kid your age might need God's help and protection? (During a thunderstorm. When going to a new school. When standing up for what's right.)

3. What are some ways to show your joy and celebrate God's help and protection? (Sing songs of praise to God. Pray to God, thanking Him for all He has done. Tell others about how God helps and protects His people.)

4. Why do you think praising God brings us joy? (We are happy that He has cared for us and promises always to care for us. It pleases God when we praise Him. It reminds us of His love and faithfulness. It makes us love Him more.)

Additional Information for Older Children

George Chen spent 18 years in the prison. When he was set free, he helped Chinese Christians start new churches and tell other people about Jesus. During the years George was in prison, the government killed many Chinese Christians who were not in prison. George thanked God that because he was in prison for so long, he was kept alive, and he could continue to obey God after he was set free.

Music Man

Knowing that Jesus is God's Son and that Jesus makes it possible for us to be part of God's family gives us joy.

Teacher's Materials

Bible with bookmark at Psalm 95:1, keyboard or other musical instrument; optional—CD or cassette of Keith Green's music and player.

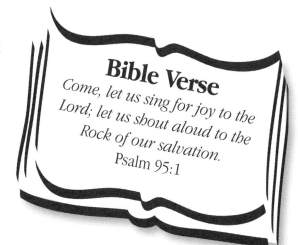

Bible Verse

Come, let us sing for joy to the Lord; let us shout aloud to the Rock of our salvation.
Psalm 95:1

Introduce the Object Talk

We can have joy because we know that Jesus is God's Son and that He makes it possible for us to be part of God's family. Let's find out how one person was joyful because of what he knew about Jesus.

Present the Object Talk

1. Show and/or play keyboard or other musical instrument. **What musical instrument do any of you play? How often do you practice your instrument? What do you like most about playing your instrument?** Volunteers answer.

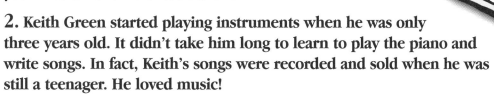

2. Keith Green started playing instruments when he was only three years old. It didn't take him long to learn to play the piano and write songs. In fact, Keith's songs were recorded and sold when he was still a teenager. He loved music!

When Keith grew up, he became a Christian. Knowing about Jesus' love made Keith so joyful that he wanted to love and obey God and to tell everyone he could about Jesus. Keith and his wife, Melody, spent almost every night leading Bible studies for people who had no homes, drug addicts and other people who needed help. But then, because of his love for God, Keith decided to write and sing songs to tell people about Jesus and how to follow Him.

When Keith was 28 years old, he died in a plane crash. Many of the songs he wrote are still sung today because they tell the truth about what it means to love and obey Jesus. (Optional: Play one or more of Keith Green's songs.) **It's sad to know that Keith Green died, but as Christians we can have joy because we know that Keith is in heaven with a living Jesus.**

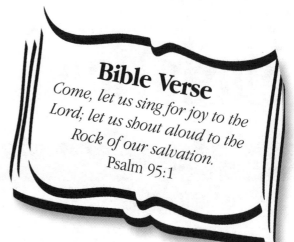

Bible Verse
Come, let us sing for joy to the Lord; let us shout aloud to the Rock of our salvation.
Psalm 95:1

Conclude

Read Psalm 95:1 aloud. **What are some ways Keith Green showed he felt joyful because of what he knew about Jesus?** Children respond. **Let's thank God for Jesus.** Lead children in prayer. Talk with interested children about becoming members of God's family (refer to "Leading a Child to Christ" article on p. 12).

Discussion Questions

1. **Psalm 95:1 tells us to "sing for joy to the Lord." When have you sung for joy? How is singing for joy different from singing because you have to?**

2. **What do you know about Jesus that makes you joyful?**

3. **What are some other ways to show that we are joyful because Jesus is God's Son and makes it possible for us to be part of God's family?**

Additional Information for Older Children

When Keith and Melody Green first became Christians, they lived in a small house. Many people came to their house to hear about Jesus and learn about Jesus' love for them. Pretty soon their small house was overflowing with people and they were running out of space! So Keith and Melody bought the house next door, and when that house became too crowded, they rented five more houses on nearby streets!

Sing a Song

Worship God with joy because of the great things He has done.

Teacher's Materials

Bible with bookmark at Psalm 100:2, cassette/CD recording of "Hark! the Herald Angels Sing" and player or photocopies of words and music, large sheet of paper, marker.

Bible Verse

Worship the Lord with gladness; come before him with joyful songs. Psalm 100:2

Introduce the Object Talk

God has done so many great things! We can joyfully worship God when we think about the great things God has done. Let's find out about one man who worshiped God and helped others worship God, too.

Present the Object Talk

1. Invite children to sing "Hark! the Herald Angels Sing" or listen to song on cassette/CD. **When do we usually sing this song? What does this song say about Jesus?** Children respond. **A man named Charles Wesley wrote this song and many other songs about Jesus.**

2. Charles Wesley grew up in a very big family in England in the 1700s. He went to church and did many good things all his life, but he didn't really understand what it meant to be a Christian or how much God loved him.

When Charles was a grown-up, he lived with some Christians in London. While he was there, Charles saw how kind and gentle they were, and he heard them talk about how they lived as part of God's family. Those Christians helped Charles understand God's love for him.

Charles was so glad to know of God's love that he began to write songs about God's love and forgiveness. For many years Charles and his brother, John, preached and sang about God's

love and forgiveness to people all over England. Charles eventually wrote 6,000 hymns! Many people learned to love and worship God because of Charles's music and preaching.

Conclude

Read Psalm 100:2 aloud. **How did Charles Wesley show his joy for the great things God has done?** (He wrote and sang songs about God.) **What are some things God has done for which you are thankful?** List children's responses on a large sheet of paper. Lead children in prayer, thanking God for items children listed.

Bible Verse

Worship the Lord with gladness; come before him with joyful songs. Psalm 100:2

Discussion Questions

1. **How do people often show that they are joyful or happy?** (Smile. Sing.)

2. **How can we show joy when we worship God?** (Sing songs that tell of God's greatness. Tell others about the ways in which God helps us. Thank God in prayer for the good things He gives us.)

3. **What is one way we have worshiped God today?**

Additional Information for Older Children

"Hark! the Herald Angels Sing" is often sung to celebrate Jesus' birth. Another of the hymns Charles Wesley wrote is often sung to celebrate Jesus' resurrection. Ask volunteers to take turns reading one or more stanzas of "Christ the Lord Is Risen Today." **What words from this song help us tell about our joy that Jesus is alive?**

Freeing the Slaves

Patiently continue to help others in the best ways you can.

Teacher's Materials
Bible with bookmark at Psalm 106:3, book of rules (game rule book, driver's manual, etc.).

Introduce the Object Talk
Even when it's hard, patiently continue to help others in the best ways possible. Let's find out about a man who was known for patiently helping others for many, many years.

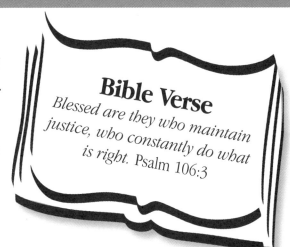

Bible Verse
Blessed are they who maintain justice, who constantly do what is right. Psalm 106:3

Present the Object Talk
1. Show book you brought. **What does this book tell about?** (Rules for [playing chess].) **Why do you think rules are important?** Children tell ideas. **William Wilberforce's job was making rules. He was a member of Parliament in England from 1780 to 1825. (That's like being a member of Congress in the United States.)**

DMV Rules of the Road

2. After William became a member of God's family, he realized that he could serve God and show his love for Him by doing his best to help others through his job in Parliament.

In 1788, William made a long speech in Parliament. He asked the other people in Parliament to make a new law to end slavery. Many people didn't want to hear that slavery was wrong because they made a lot of money from selling slaves and from the work slaves did. Parliament voted down William's idea, but William didn't give up. Every year for 18 years, William tried to convince people to end slavery.

Finally, Parliament decided to pass a law that made it illegal to force people to be slaves. But there were still many people who were already slaves, and the new law didn't set them free, so William's job wasn't over! He patiently kept working to free slaves until the end of his life. Just four days before William died, Parliament passed a law saying that ALL slavery was illegal in England and in all the British colonies.

Conclude

Read Psalm 106:3 aloud. **This verse says that God is pleased when people do what is right to help others. How did William Wilberforce help others?** (He asked people to pass laws to end slavery.) Lead children in prayer, asking God to help them do their best to help others.

Bible Verse
Blessed are they who maintain justice, who constantly do what is right. Psalm 106:3

Discussion Questions

1. When might it be hard to help others? (When you're tired. When you have your own jobs to do.)

2. How can you remember to patiently do your best to help others? (Ask God's help. Remember God's patience.)

3. What are some things you can do to help others this week?

Additional Information for Older Children

After William Wilberforce became a member of God's family, he considered leaving Parliament to become a pastor or doing something else to serve God. His friends convinced him that he could serve God by staying in Parliament and passing laws that would help others. In addition to working to end slavery, William helped people get a good education and helped missionaries travel to other countries.

A Faithful Watchman

God showed His faithfulness in keeping His promise to send the Savior.

Teacher's Materials

Bible with bookmark at Psalm 117:1,2; one or more items security guards use (flashlight, keys, billy club, walkie talkie, handcuffs, etc.).

Introduce the Object Talk

God showed His faithfulness when He kept His promise to send Jesus to be our Savior. Let's find out about someone who trusted God's faithfulness and was faithful to God.

Bible Verse

Praise the Lord, all you nations; extol him, all you peoples. For great is his love toward us, and the faithfulness of the Lord endures forever. Psalm 117:1,2

Present the Object Talk

1. Show items you brought. **Watchmen, or security guards, use things like these to help them protect buildings and people and make sure that they are safe. Just like watchmen watch for problems and tell people what they need to know to be safe, preachers pray for people and tell them what they need to know to become members of God's family and be saved from sin's punishment.**

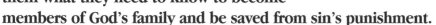

2. In the early 1920s, a man in China changed his name from Ni Shu-tsu to Watchman Nee. He chose this name because his mother had prayed for him to be born while she listened to the night watchman make his rounds. When Ni Shu-tsu heard that his mother promised God that her son would love and obey Him, Ni Shu-tsu decided that the name Watchman would remind him and others of his plan to serve God.

For the rest of his life, Watchman did his best to be faithful in obeying God. One day Watchman got a letter asking him to preach in the city of Chien-O. He wanted to go, but the boat trip to Chien-O cost 80 dollars and Watchman only had 10 dollars. Watchman asked for God's help and then went to the river. There was a small boat going to Chien-O for only seven dollars! Watchman Nee's faithful dependence on God meant others could hear about God.

Conclude

Read Psalm 117:1,2 aloud. **What do these verses tell us about God? How did Watchman Nee show he was faithful to God?** (He obeyed God, even when he didn't know how God would provide for him.) Lead children in prayer, thanking God for His faithfulness.

Bible Verse

Praise the Lord, all you nations; extol him, all you peoples. For great is his love toward us, and the faithfulness of the Lord endures forever. Psalm 117:1,2

Discussion Questions

1. How has God shown faithfulness to us? (He kept His promise to send Jesus. He makes us part of His family when we trust in Him. He keeps His promises to love and be with us.) Talk with interested children about becoming members of God's family (refer to "Leading a Child to Christ" article on p. 12).

2. When might people today have a hard time trusting God's faithfulness? What could you say or do to encourage someone in a situation like this?

3. How does knowing about God's faithfulness help us? (We can depend on Him.)

Additional Information for Older Children

During the same year he became a Christian, Watchman Nee began writing books and articles for newspapers. Many Christians still read and learn from Watchman Nee's books. In 1952, Watchman Nee was arrested and put in prison because of his belief in God. He died in prison on March 30, 1972.

The Shelter

God's Word helps us learn how to have self-control and live wisely.

Teacher's Materials

Bible with bookmark at Psalm 119:133, umbrella.

Introduce the Object Talk

God's Word helps us learn how to have self-control and live wisely. Listen to find out about one man and his family who helped others learn about God's Word, too!

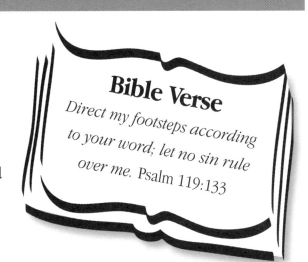

Bible Verse

Direct my footsteps according to your word; let no sin rule over me. Psalm 119:133

Present the Object Talk

1. Show umbrella. **When do people use this? Why?** Children respond. **People use an umbrella for shelter from rain and snow. A man named Francis Schaeffer and his family named their home in Switzerland L'Abri (lah-BREE), the French word for "shelter." Why might you call a home a shelter?** (Keeps you safe.)

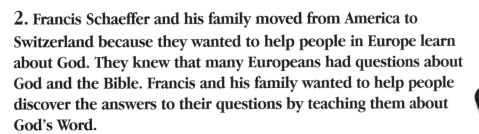

2. Francis Schaeffer and his family moved from America to Switzerland because they wanted to help people in Europe learn about God. They knew that many Europeans had questions about God and the Bible. Francis and his family wanted to help people discover the answers to their questions by teaching them about God's Word.

The Schaeffer family made their house, L'Abri, a place where people from around the world could come and study God's Word. They prayed that God would send to L'Abri people who had questions about God. While the Schaeffers' guests lived at L'Abri, they saw how people who loved God lived each day. The Schaeffers helped their guests learn wisdom from the Bible. Many of these guests became convinced that God is real and that His Word tells the best way to live.

Conclude

Read Psalm 119:133 aloud. **What does it mean for God to "direct [your] footsteps according to [His] word"?** (He will help you obey the Bible.) **What did the Schaeffer family do that showed they obeyed God's Word?** (They opened their home to teach others about God.) **God's Word teaches us wise ways to live, and as we follow these wise ways, we learn to have self-control.** Lead children in prayer, thanking God for His Word that tells us wise ways to live.

Bible Verse
Direct my footsteps according to your word; let no sin rule over me. Psalm 119:133

Discussion Questions

1. What are some of the ways God's Word tells us to live? (Love and forgive others. Ask Jesus to forgive our sins. Pray to God and ask for help with our problems. Tell the good news about Jesus to other people.)

2. What is one way you can obey God's Word this week? Share your own answer with your children before asking children to respond.

Additional Information for Older Children

When Francis Schaeffer was a teenager, he decided that he didn't know if God really existed or not. Francis began to read the Bible to find out if God is real or not. Francis started reading in the book of Genesis. After reading the Bible, Francis became convinced that God is real. Francis also believed that the Bible is God's Word. Francis became a Christian when he was 18 years old, and for the rest of his life he helped others learn to believe in God.

Faith of a Mother

The habits we form by being faithful to God help us do what is right, even when trouble comes.

Teacher's Materials
Bible with bookmark at Proverbs 3:3, clock with hour and minute hands.

Introduce the Object Talk
The habits we form by being faithful to God help us do what is right at all times. Let's look at some different things we can do with our time.

Bible Verse
Let love and faithfulness never leave you; bind them around your neck, write them on the tablet of your heart. Proverbs 3:3

Present the Object Talk
1. Show clock. **How long does it take for the short hand to move from one number to another?** Children respond. **What are some things you can do in an hour?** (Watch [two] cartoon shows. Drive to [a location approximately 60 miles away]. Attend soccer practice.)

2. One person who lived a long time ago had a habit of doing something for two hours every day. Susanna Wesley, a woman who lived in England in the 1700s, prayed for two hours every day. Even though Susanna had many children to take care of and was very busy with all kinds of work, every day she stopped whatever she was doing to pray and think about God's Word for one hour in the morning and one hour in the evening. Susanna began this habit of showing love and obedience to God when her children were young, and she faithfully continued the habit throughout her life. She had two sons who not only became famous preachers and songwriters but also were people God used to tell the good news of Jesus all over England!

Conclude

Read Proverbs 3:3 aloud. **What are some habits Proverbs 3:3 talks about?** (Showing love and being faithful to God.) **How did Susanna Wesley obey this verse?** (She prayed and thought about God's Word every day.) **What are some other habits that show love and faithfulness to God?** Lead children in prayer, thanking God for His love and asking for His help in showing love and faithfulness to Him.

Bible Verse

Let love and faithfulness never leave you; bind them around your neck, write them on the tablet of your heart. *Proverbs 3:3*

Discussion Questions

1. When you "bind [something] around your neck" or "write [it] on the tablet of your heart" (know it by heart), it means you are trying to keep that thing close to you so that you will never lose it. What is Proverbs 3:3 telling us not to lose? (Love and faithfulness to God.)

2. What does it mean to be faithful to God? (To love Him with all your heart, soul, mind and strength. To obey God's commands no matter what.)

3. What kinds of habits could you form that would show your faithfulness to God? (Reading the Bible to learn more about God. Praying to God every day. Obeying God's commands.)

4. How can these habits help you when things are hard? (Knowing God's Word will help a person know the right thing to do, even in difficult situations. Praying to God will be comforting in times of fear or sadness.)

Additional Information for Older Children

One of Susanna Wesley's sons, Charles Wesley, wrote many songs called hymns that are still sung in churches today. (Optional: Use bookmarks or Post-it Notes to mark several of Charles Wesley's hymns in some church hymnals: "Love Divine, All Loves Excelling," "Hark! the Herald Angels Sing," "Jesus, Lover of My Soul," "O for a Thousand Tongues to Sing," "Christ the Lord Is Risen Today," etc. Children find and read some of the songs. **Can you find words or phrases that remind you of showing love? Of being faithful?**)

It Is Well

Rely on God's wisdom and show patience, even when bad things that we don't understand happen.

Teacher's Materials

Bible with bookmark at Proverbs 3:5, sheet of paper, pencil; optional—hymnbook with "It Is Well with My Soul," a musician to lead children in singing the hymn.

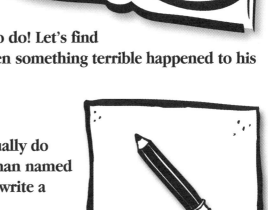

Bible Verse

Trust in the Lord with all your heart and lean not on your own understanding. Proverbs 3:5

Introduce the Object Talk

When bad things happen that we don't understand, sometimes the hardest thing to do is trust God's wisdom and show patience. But that is actually the best thing to do! Let's find out how one man trusted God's wisdom when something terrible happened to his family.

Present the Object Talk

1. Hold up paper and pencil. **What do you usually do with these two objects?** Children respond. **A man named Horatio Spafford used a pencil and paper to write a poem to express how he was feeling.**

2. In 1873, Horatio Spafford sent his wife and four daughters ahead of him on a ship to Europe while he completed some unexpected business. Soon he got a message from his wife that the ship had sunk and all of their daughters died. Only his wife was saved. Horatio quickly got on a ship and sailed to meet his wife. As his ship was passing the spot where his daughters had drowned, Horatio went out on the deck and wrote these words: "When sorrows like sea billows roll—Whatever my lot, Thou hast taught me to say, It is well, it is well with my soul." (Optional: Read entire first verse of the hymn aloud.)

3. What do you think he meant by writing "it is well with my soul"? Children respond. **Horatio wrote that whether he felt peace or sorrow, he trusted God. People were so impressed with the words of Horatio's poem that they put the**

poem to music and it became a popular hymn which people still sing today.
(Optional: Musician leads children in singing hymn.)

Bible Verse
Trust in the Lord with all your heart and lean not on your own understanding. Proverbs 3:5

Conclude

Read Proverbs 3:5 aloud. **How did Horatio Spafford show he trusted in God, even when bad things happened to him?** (He wrote a song about loving and trusting God.) Lead children in prayer, thanking God that we can trust Him with our problems, no matter how bad the problems are.

Discussion Questions

1. What might help you show patience during hard times? (Talking to God about the situation. Praying and asking God for patience. Reading the Bible to find out how God helped people in all kinds of hard situations.)

2. How does knowing that God is wise make it easier to be patient in hard times? (God knows what we need and will give it to us at just the right time. He plans everything for our good. He has a reason for everything.)

3. What are some things you can do to remember God's wisdom in order to help you show patience? (Talk to God. Read about how God helped people in the Bible. Talk to others about times they relied on God's wisdom.)

Additional Information for Older Children

After the accident, the Spaffords moved to Israel and had more children. Mrs. Spafford decided to do everything she could to save other children. One day a Muslim man whose wife had died came and asked Mrs. Spafford to raise his newborn baby. Soon many people were bringing her children whose parents had left them, and Spafford's Children's Home began. God helped the Spaffords raise as many as 60 children at a time!

Faithful Friendship

Faithfulness to others means being a friend in good and bad times.

Teacher's Materials
Bible with bookmark at Proverbs 17:17, sleeping bag or pillow.

Introduce the Object Talk
Showing faithfulness means being a good friend no matter what—in good and bad times. Let's find out how one man showed he was a faithful friend.

Bible Verse
A friend loves at all times.
Proverbs 17:17

Present the Object Talk
1. Show sleeping bag or pillow. **When do you use this?** (Camping. Sleeping overnight at a friend's house.) **One way to show friendship is to stay overnight at a friend's house. One man showed friendship by doing more than staying overnight with his friends. This man chose to live with the people that he wanted to be friends with.**

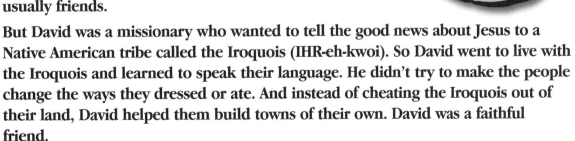

2. David Zeisberger lived in the 1800s. During that time many Native Americans were being cheated out of the land they lived on. White people and Native Americans weren't usually friends.

But David was a missionary who wanted to tell the good news about Jesus to a Native American tribe called the Iroquois (IHR-eh-kwoi). So David went to live with the Iroquois and learned to speak their language. He didn't try to make the people change the ways they dressed or ate. And instead of cheating the Iroquois out of their land, David helped them build towns of their own. David was a faithful friend.

Later when the members of David's church wanted to become missionaries to the Iroquois, the tribe didn't want these missionaries to come. White people had cheated them too many times! But one of the Iroquois called David a friend and a brother. Others who knew David agreed that David had proven to be a fair and faithful friend to the Iroquois people. He had even gone to jail instead of giving up his friendship with them. Because of David's friendship, the Iroquois allowed the missionaries to tell them about Jesus.

Bible Verse
A friend loves at all times.
Proverbs 17:17

Conclude

Read Proverbs 17:17 aloud. **Someone who is faithful shows friendship in good and bad times. How did David Zeisberger show faithfulness to his friends?** (He learned their language. He helped them build towns.) **Let's thank God for being faithful to us and loving us at all times.** Lead children in prayer. Talk with interested children about becoming members of God's family (refer to "Leading a Child to Christ" article on p. 12).

Discussion Questions

1. Who has been a faithful friend to you? What has this person done to show friendship to you?

2. When is it hard to show friendship to others?

3. How can you be a good friend to someone who has a hard time learning at school or to someone who has a hard time getting along with others?

4. Why might kids your age have a hard time continuing to be a faithful friend to someone? (When that person moves away. When he or she stops being nice. When we find new friends.) **What can we do to remember to be faithful friends, even when it's hard?** (Ask God's help. Remember the words of Proverbs 17:17.)

Additional Information for Older Children

David Zeisberger was such a good friend to the Native Americans that one tribe even adopted him into their tribe. This tribe called David Zeisberger their brother and gave him a Native-American name. (Optional: Print the name of the tribe, "Onandag," and the name they gave David Zeisberger, "Ganousaracherie," on a large sheet of paper. Show paper to children.) **Because David was adopted into this tribe, many other tribes also welcomed him as their friend.**

Bible Translators

Have a gentle attitude so that you can learn wisdom from God and others who love Him.

Teacher's Materials

Bible with bookmark at Proverbs 19:20, object representing something a friend has taught you or helped you with (golf club, crocheted blanket, paintbrush, pie tin, etc.).

Bible Verse

Listen to advice and accept instruction, and in the end you will be wise. Proverbs 19:20

Introduce the Object Talk

Having a gentle attitude helps us learn wisdom from God and others who love Him. Let's listen to find out how one man's gentle attitude helped him learn something that helped people all over the world.

Present the Object Talk

1. Show and describe object. **I brought this (golf club) because my friend (Sam) helped me learn how to (play golf). What is something a friend has helped you learn?** Children respond. **A man named Cameron Townsend went to Guatemala as a missionary. He was very glad to find a friend there to help him out!**

2. When Cameron first went to Guatemala, whenever he met people with whom he wanted to talk about God, he'd ask, "Do you know the Lord Jesus?" But when he asked this question in Spanish, it translated as, "Do you know Mr. Jesus (hay-SOOS)?" Because Jesus is a common Hispanic name, the people he was talking to did not know Cameron was talking about Jesus the Son of God. He also discovered that many of the people he talked to did not even know Spanish but spoke other languages. There were hundreds of different languages in that area!

Cameron wondered how he would be able to talk to these people about Jesus, so he prayed for God's help. Soon Cameron met an Indian named Francisco Diaz (FRAHN-sees-koh DEE-ahz) who loved God, too. Francisco taught Cameron his language and helped him translate the New Testament into that language. Cameron was so excited about this idea of translating the Scriptures into everyone's own

language that he began an organization called Wycliffe Bible Translators. Today Wycliffe missionaries help people all over the world learn about God in their own language, all because of God's help and Cameron Townsend's willingness to learn from Francisco Diaz.

Bible Verse

Listen to advice and accept instruction, and in the end you will be wise. Proverbs 19:20

Conclude

Read Proverbs 19:20 aloud. **This verse describes what someone who has a gentle attitude is like. What did Cameron Townsend learn because he had a gentle attitude and accepted instruction?** (He learned to speak the language of the people he wanted to help.) Lead children in prayer, asking God's help in learning from others.

Discussion Questions

1. What other words can you use to describe someone who has a gentle attitude? ("Listens." "Humble." "Peaceful." "Respectful." "Unselfish.")

2. Why does having a gentle attitude lead to wisdom? (Listening to others is a way to learn from them.) Ask a volunteer to read Proverbs 19:20 aloud.

3. Who are some good people to learn from? (Parents. People who love God. Teachers. Pastors.) **What can you learn from (teachers) when you have a gentle attitude?** (How to love God and others. Right choices and ways to obey God.)

4. What are some ways you can get instructions from God? (Read God's Word. Pray to Him. Talk to other people who love God.)

Additional Information for Older Children

Wycliffe Bible missionaries have translated the New Testament into over 500 languages, and they work in over 70 countries. The average translation job takes 10 to 20 years! (Optional: Invite someone who has served with Wycliffe to talk to your children, or find additional information at www.wycliffe.org.)

Escape from Germany

Acting in ways that demonstrate belief in God shows faithfulness.

Teacher's Materials
Bible with bookmark at Proverbs 20:11, star cut from yellow construction paper or fabric.

Introduce the Object Talk
When we're faithful to God, it means that our actions and words show obedience to God. Let's find out how one person showed His faithfulness to God in a very difficult and scary time.

Bible Verse
Even a child is known by his actions, by whether his conduct is pure and right. Proverbs 20:11

Present the Object Talk
1. Show yellow star. **When people called Nazis were in control of Germany during World War II, Jewish people were forced to wear stars like this on their clothes. The Nazis wanted everyone to hate Jewish people. Not all of the German people agreed with the Nazis. A German man named Dietrich (DEE-trihk) Bonhoeffer (BAHN-hahf-uhr) dared to help people who wore yellow stars.**

2. Dietrich Bonhoeffer was a pastor in Germany during World War II. Many other German pastors would not help Jewish people, because they were afraid of Hitler and the Nazi army, but Dietrich said that this was not right!

Dietrich did more than just say that it was wrong to hate Jewish people; he did what he could to help them. One time Dietrich helped a group of Jewish people escape from Germany. He had papers that gave him permission to travel in and out of Germany. On one trip, he took some Jews with him. German guards stopped the car, but because of his permission papers, the guards let him leave Germany—along with the Jewish people in his car. Later, the Nazis found out what he was doing and arrested him. While he was in prison, Dietrich wrote several books about faithfully serving God. Dietrich was eventually killed because of his actions that showed his belief in God. People today still read the books he wrote and remember how important it is to be faithful to do what is right.

Conclude

Read Proverbs 20:11 aloud. **What are some actions that showed Pastor Bonhoeffer's belief in God? How did this pastor's actions make a difference?** Lead children in prayer, asking God to help them be faithful in showing belief in God.

Bible Verse

Even a child is known by his actions, by whether his conduct is pure and right. Proverbs 20:11

Discussion Questions

1. How do kids your age show that they believe in God? (Don't go along with the crowd in doing wrong. Go to church. Read their Bibles. Pray and ask God for help when they have problems. Treat others kindly.)

2. How do you think your faithfulness to God might help another person?

3. When are some times you have seen other people show their belief in God? Briefly share your own answer before you ask for responses from children.

4. How can you show faithfulness to God when you are with your friends? When you are with your family?

Additional Information for Older Children

While in prison, Deitrich wrote many letters. His letters to the woman he was planning to marry were collected into a book called *Love Letters from Cell 92.* On the day Deitrich was killed, the prison doctor saw him praying in his cell. The doctor later said that in all his years as a doctor, he had never seen anyone more faithful about doing God's will.

Anger Control

God can help us control angry feelings so that we can treat others in ways that please Him.

Teacher's Materials

Bible with bookmark at Proverbs 29:11, month-by-month calendar; optional—copy of "I Have a Dream" speech by Dr. Martin Luther King, Jr. (available from library or on the Internet).

Bible Verse

A fool gives full vent to his anger, but a wise man keeps himself under control. Proverbs 29:11

Introduce the Object Talk

With God's help, we can treat others in ways that please Him, even when we're angry. Let's find out what one man did to control angry feelings.

Present the Object Talk

1. Show calendar. Invite several volunteers to find favorite holidays listed on the calendar. **What or whom do these holidays help us to remember?** Children tell. **Martin Luther King, Jr., is a man whose actions are remembered each year by many people.**

2. Martin Luther King, Jr., Day is celebrated each year on the third Monday of January. What do you know about Dr. King? Volunteers respond. Supplement children's information as needed with the following information: **In 1954, Dr. King became the pastor of a church in Alabama. At this time many African-American people felt very angry, because they weren't being treated fairly. Dr. King was angry, too. Dr. King believed that because God loves everyone the same, all people should be treated fairly.**

Even though he was angry, Martin Luther King, Jr., didn't let his angry feelings cause him to treat others in unkind ways. Instead, he led marches to call attention to unfairness. He gave speeches and preached sermons, telling people to treat each other fairly. Dr. King asked government leaders to pass laws so that African-Americans

would be treated fairly. He also warned people to do what was right at all times and to treat others in ways that pleased **God.** (Optional: Read aloud part of Dr. King's "I Have a Dream" speech.)

Conclude

Read Proverbs 29:11 aloud. **What does Proverbs 29:11 say a wise man does?** Volunteer answers. **When we keep our words and actions under control, it means** we think about and plan our words and actions so that they show love and obedience to God. **What is a way Martin Luther King, Jr., showed he had self-control?** (He didn't treat others in unkind ways, even when he was angry. He taught others to do right and please God.) Lead children in prayer, asking God to help them show self-control.

Bible Verse

A fool gives full vent to his anger, but a wise man keeps himself under control. Proverbs 29:11

Discussion Questions

1. **When are some times it is hard for kids your age to control their anger?**

2. **What are some things people do to help control their anger?** (Count to 10. Take a deep breath. Walk away. Tell God about their anger. Ask God's help in being kind.)

3. **Why do you think it is wise to control your anger?**

Additional Information for Older Children

In 1964, Martin Luther King, Jr., won the Nobel Peace Prize. Every year, beginning in 1901, money set aside by a Swedish inventor, Alfred Nobel, is divided; and five prizes are given away to people who have worked hard to help others. There are awards for the most important discovery or invention in physics, chemistry and medicine as well as awards for literature and working for international peace. Martin Luther King, Jr., won the prize for peace because he taught others to live peacefully with each other.

Joy in Salvation

God's gift of salvation brings great joy.

Teacher's Materials

Bible with bookmark at Habakkuk 3:18, shoe box with shoes inside.

Introduce the Object Talk

When we accept God's gift of salvation, it brings us great joy. Let's find out how one person learned about the joy that comes with God's gift of salvation.

Bible Verse

I will rejoice in the Lord, I will be joyful in God my Savior. Habakkuk 3:18

Present the Object Talk

1. Show shoe box. **When have you gone to a store to buy new shoes? How did a salesperson help you?** Children respond. **Dwight Moody was a successful shoe salesman in Boston, but one day his shoe sales didn't go as planned.**

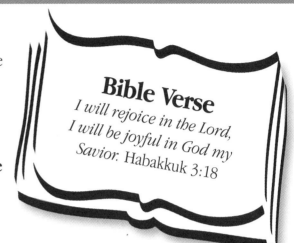

2. Dwight grew up in a very poor family. Dwight hated being poor and was determined to become rich. When he was 17 years old, he went to live with his Uncle Samuel in Boston. He worked in his uncle's shoe store. Soon Dwight was making a lot of money, because he was one of the best shoe salesmen around.

School teacher, Mr. Kimball, visited Dwight at the shoe store. Dwight thought that his teacher had come to buy shoes. But Mr. Kimball did more than that—right there in the store he invited Dwight to become a member of God's family! Dwight did. He said he felt a new kind of happiness and love and everything was different. Now Dwight knew that true joy came from being a part of God's family! Dwight didn't want to keep his joy a secret. He went back home to visit his family to tell them about Jesus, too. And for the rest of his life, Dwight spent most of his time telling people about Jesus and the joy that comes from being a Christian.

Bible Verse
*I will rejoice in the Lord,
I will be joyful in God my
Savior.* Habakkuk 3:18

Conclude
Read Habakkuk 3:18 aloud. **How did Dwight Moody show he was joyful to know Jesus?** (He wanted to tell his family and other people about Jesus.) **Let's thank God for His gift of salvation.** Lead children in prayer.

Discussion Questions
1. **What are some reasons we have to "be joyful in God"? What are some reasons we have for being thankful to God?**

2. **What are some of the ways people hear about God's gift of salvation and the joy it brings?** (Friends tell them. They go to church. They read the Bible.)

3. **The Bible tells us that God is joyful when we become a part of His family. Why?** (He loves us and wants us to be part of His family.)

4. **When we hear about God and accept God's gift of salvation by becoming members of God's family, we experience joy. Why?** (Our sins are forgiven by God. We can have eternal life. We know God loves us.) Talk with interested children about becoming members of God's family (refer to "Leading a Child to Christ" article on p. 12).

Additional Information for Older Children
Dwight Moody became known as a man who tried to honor and obey God in all his actions. Dwight traveled all over America and England to preach about Jesus. Many people learned about Jesus through his preaching. People today still learn about Jesus from organizations Dwight helped to start, such as the Moody Bible Institute and Moody Press in Chicago.

Good Soup

Listening to others and treating them fairly are ways to show God's goodness.

Teacher's Materials

Bible with bookmark at Zechariah 7:9, can of soup.

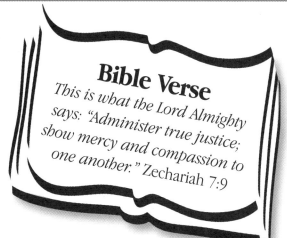

Bible Verse

This is what the Lord Almighty says: "Administer true justice; show mercy and compassion to one another." Zechariah 7:9

Introduce the Object Talk

God's goodness shows in our lives when we listen to others and treat them fairly. Let's find out how one man showed God's goodness in the way he treated others.

Present the Object Talk

1. Show can of soup. **When do you like to eat soup? What kinds of soup do you like best?** Volunteers tell. **One man was not happy when he saw some poor-tasting soup that was being served in his city.**

2. Charles Tindley was born as a slave in 1856, just a few years before Abraham Lincoln set the slaves free. When he grew up, Charles became the pastor of a church in the city of Philadelphia. Charles worried about some poor people who lived on the streets instead of in homes. He wanted to treat them in good ways, and he wanted to teach them about Jesus.

One day Charles went to a kitchen where poor people were given soup and bread to eat. But when Charles looked at the food, he saw that the soup was very watery and the bread was stale. Charles felt sorry for the people and wanted them to receive better food.

The next Sunday, Charles told his congregation that they were going to help the poor people in their city. The church members cooked good, healthy food and welcomed the poor people into their church. Charles often talked to the poor people and showed how much he cared about them. Many of these people considered Charles their own pastor because he cared enough to listen to them and treat them in good ways.

Conclude

Read Zechariah 7:9 aloud. **When we "administer true justice," it means we treat others fairly. What else does this verse say God wants us to do?** Children respond. **How did Charles Tindley show mercy and compassion to others?** (He helped poor people have good food to eat.) Lead children in prayer, asking God to help them listen to others and treat others fairly.

Bible Verse

This is what the Lord Almighty says: "Administer true justice; show mercy and compassion to one another." Zechariah 7:9

Discussion Questions

1. When are some times it might be hard for you to listen to others? How does listening to someone help a person know the best ways to help? (By listening, a person can learn what is really needed and what to pray for.)

2. What does it mean to treat other people fairly? (Respect each person. Care for all people in the same way you care for the people you like most.) **What can you do to treat your brother or sister more fairly? Kids at school?**

3. How can listening to others and treating them fairly help them see God's goodness? (It shows them that God thinks each person is important.)

4. What are some other ways that your actions can show God's goodness?

Additional Information for Older Children

When Charles Tindley was a boy, his father was very poor, so Charles worked for farmers doing chores. As he grew up, he had to work so much that he was unable to go to school. But Charles wanted to learn to read. He collected newspaper pages that other people had thrown away, and he slowly taught himself how to read. Then Charles was able to read the only book he had—the Bible.

School Uniforms

Look for ways to be kind to and care for others.

Teacher's Materials
Bible with bookmark at Matthew 5:7, uniform from a school or sports team.

Introduce the Object Talk
It is important to always look for opportunities in which we can be kind to and care for others. Let's find out some ways one woman found to be kind to and care for others.

Bible Verse
Blessed are the merciful, for they will be shown mercy.
Matthew 5:7

Present the Object Talk
1. Show uniform. (Optional: Volunteer wears uniform.) **When do kids your age wear uniforms?** Children tell. **In the early 1900s, school children in China wore uniforms. Schools even had contests to see which school had the best uniform.**

The children in one school, however, were embarrassed because they did not have uniforms like other children. This school was so poor the teachers could hardly buy school supplies. And because the children in the school were orphans (their parents were no longer alive), they couldn't afford to buy uniforms.

2. Grace Chang was a missionary teacher at this school. She cared for the children at the school so much that she decided to help them get uniforms. Grace planned to use her sewing machine to make the uniforms, but she didn't have any cloth! Grace prayed and asked God to help her.

God answered Grace's prayer. Soon another missionary gave her some cloth, and Grace started sewing uniforms for the children. Then Grace got women in a nearby village to help make cloth shoes for all the children. (At that time, Chinese children typically wore cloth shoes.)

Soon the jackets, skirts and shoes were ready. The children excitedly wore their uniforms to school. And when they won the contest for the best uniform, the children were even more pleased!

Bible Verse
Blessed are the merciful, for they will be shown mercy.
Matthew 5:7

Conclude

Read Matthew 5:7 aloud. **When we show mercy to others, it means we are kind to them—even when they don't deserve it. How did Grace Chang show mercy and kindness to others?** Children tell ideas. **Let's ask God to help us find ways to be kind and care for others this week.** Close in prayer.

Discussion Questions

1. Grace Chang used her sewing machine to be kind to others. What could you use to be kind to someone?

2. When has someone been kind to you? Why do you think that person chose to be kind? How did you feel as a result of that kindness?

3. Who are some people you could be kind to and care for this week?

Additional Information for Older Children

Grace Chang trusted that God would help her show kindness to others. Once, another missionary became ill and needed someone to take her home to the United States. Grace was asked to help her, but neither woman had any money for the boat ride! Grace prayed and prayed and then felt sure God wanted her to borrow money from a bank. Even though Grace had nothing to give the bank in return, the bank manager loaned her the money!

A Ship in Danger

Because we've experienced God's great love for us, we can show compassion to others.

Teacher's Materials

Bible with bookmark at Luke 10:27, toy boat or picture of a boat.

Introduce the Object Talk

God's love and compassion for us are great! Because we know about God's love, we can show compassion to other people. Let's find out how someone showed compassion to people on a boat.

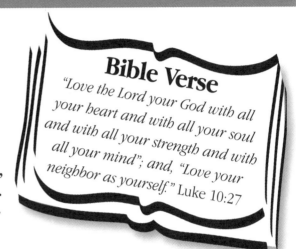

Bible Verse

"Love the Lord your God with all your heart and with all your soul and with all your strength and with all your mind"; and, "Love your neighbor as yourself." Luke 10:27

Present the Object Talk

1. Show toy boat or picture of boat. **When have you sailed on a boat? What was the weather like?** Children respond. **Sailing on a boat is fun when the weather is nice, but in cold and stormy weather, boats are dangerous places to be!**

2. One cold winter day in a sea near the country of Holland, the passengers on a boat were in big trouble. The weather was so cold that the water was beginning to freeze. The boat was getting stuck, and the people couldn't get to shore.

To make matters worse, the rescue crew from the nearest city would not help the passengers on the boat because the passengers were all members of a church the rescue crew hated. The passengers were stranded at sea!

But one man, Menno Simons, heard about the passengers on the boat. Menno belonged to a different church from the passengers, too—but he didn't let that stop him from showing God's love. Menno and some of his friends from his church decided to help the stranded passengers. Menno and his friends risked their lives in the icy water and rescued all the passengers!

Conclude

Read Luke 10:27 aloud. **What is another way to describe how this verse says we are to love God?** (We are to love God with everything we have and in every way we can.) **How did Menno Simons and his friends obey Luke 10:27?** Lead children in prayer, thanking God for His love and asking Him to help children show His love to others.

Bible Verse
"Love the Lord your God with all your heart and with all your soul and with all your strength and with all your mind"; and, "Love your neighbor as yourself." Luke 10:27

Discussion Questions

1. What does it mean to show compassion to others? (To care about others and do what you can to help them.)

2. How has God shown compassion to us? (He sent Jesus so that we could be forgiven. He promised to help us and be with us.)

3. When is a time you can show compassion to someone in your family? To your friends? When you are at school?

Additional Information for Older Children

Many government leaders in the country of the Netherlands didn't like Menno Simons and the other members of his church. They wanted to stop people from becoming members of Menno's church. The government leaders thought if they could stop Menno from telling others about God, they could stop his church from growing. They offered a reward of 100 gold coins to anyone who would tell them where Menno was. But God protected Menno. No one ever turned him in to collect the reward!

Our Daily Bread

We can have peace because God knows what we need and promises to care for us.

Teacher's Materials

Bible with bookmark at John 14:27, loaf of bread and carton of milk.

Introduce the Object Talk

God knows just what we need and He promises to take care of us! Because we can depend on God, we can have peace. Let's find out how one man showed that he had peace and trusted God.

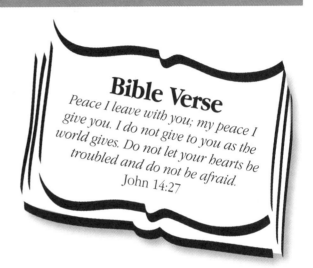

Bible Verse

Peace I leave with you; my peace I give you. I do not give to you as the world gives. Do not let your hearts be troubled and do not be afraid.
John 14:27

Present the Object Talk

1. What is your favorite breakfast food? Children respond. Show bread and milk. **People often eat bread and milk as part of their breakfast. Let's find out about some children who didn't know if they would have any food to eat for breakfast.**

2. In the early 1800s, George Müller was a preacher in England. George was also the leader of an orphanage for poor children. One morning the tables in the orphanage dining room were set, but there was no food and no money to buy food. George didn't know where he would get food for breakfast. George and the children prayed, "Dear Father, we thank You for what You are going to give us to eat."

As soon as they finished praying, the town baker knocked at the door. He had loaves of fresh bread! The baker had gotten up early to make bread because he felt that God wanted him to give this gift to the children at the orphanage.
A moment later, there was another knock at the door. The milkman's cart had broken down outside of the orphanage, and he needed to empty the cart before he could repair it. The milk would be wasted, so he

offered to give the milk to the children. Time after time, God answered George's prayers just like this! George and the orphans had peace because they trusted God's care.

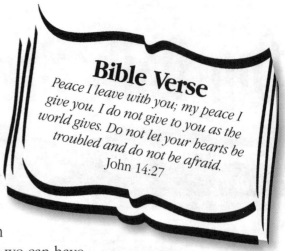

Bible Verse

Peace I leave with you; my peace I give you. I do not give to you as the world gives. Do not let your hearts be troubled and do not be afraid.
John 14:27

Conclude

Read John 14:27 aloud. **How did God care for George Müller and the orphans?** Children respond. **What are some other ways God cares for people?** Lead children in prayer, thanking God for taking care of us, so we can have peace and depend on Him.

Discussion Questions

1. What are some things a kid your age might worry about? (A test in school. A sick parent or grandparent. Being liked by others.)

2. What is something a kid can do if he or she is feeling worried about something? (Remember God's promise to care for us. Tell God what he or she is worried about. Read in God's Word about how He takes care of His family.)

3. What does Jesus tell us about worrying? (There is no need to worry, because God knows what we need and will provide for us.)

4. How can we get the peace that Jesus said He left with us? (Ask Jesus to forgive our sins and tell Him that we want to be members of God's family. Keep trusting God, even when we're worried.) Talk to interested children about salvation (see "Leading a Child to Christ" article on p. 12 in this book).

Additional Information for Older Children

Before George Müller opened his orphanage, only rich children were allowed to stay in England's orphanages. George said that he opened his orphanage for two reasons: he wanted to care for poor orphans and he wanted to show that God would supply the needs of anyone who prayed and trusted in Him. Over ten thousand boys and girls were cared for because George prayed and trusted God.

Prison Reform

We can follow Jesus' example of showing love to people others might ignore.

Teacher's Materials

Bible with bookmark at John 15:12, bag containing six to eight school supplies (pencil, notebook, eraser, ruler, pencil sharpener, crayons, folder, book, etc.).

Introduce the Object Talk

Jesus showed love to people whom other people ignored. Let's find out how one person followed Jesus' example and how we can follow His example, too.

Bible Verse
My command is this: Love each other as I have loved you.
John 15:12

Present the Object Talk

1. Show bag. **This bag is full of things you might need for school.** Invite volunteers to guess items in the bag. Show items that children correctly guess and then identify items not guessed. **A long time ago in England, some children didn't have any of these things. They didn't even have a school to go to, because they lived with their mothers in a prison. The children hadn't done anything wrong; but at that time, children had to go to prison with their mothers if they didn't have other family members to care for them.**

2. Even though most people didn't care about prisoners, a woman named Elizabeth Fry visited this prison. She was shocked by the horrible conditions in which the women and their children lived. Within a few years, Elizabeth helped to organize a school for the children and collected the school supplies they needed. Then she set up a room where the women prisoners could learn to sew.

Elizabeth also wanted the prisoners to know about Jesus' love for them. She talked about Jesus to the women and children and read from her Bible about Jesus' love and forgiveness. Elizabeth's work to help women and children in prison became so well known that people in the English government and even the queen of England, Queen Victoria, gave money to support her work.

Conclude

Read John 15:12 aloud. **How did Elizabeth Fry obey this verse?** Children respond. **Let's thank God for Jesus' example and ask Him to help us show His love to others.** Lead children in prayer.

Bible Verse
My command is this: Love each other as I have loved you.
John 15:12

Discussion Questions

1. When have you felt ignored? How did another person help you?

2. Who are some people kids your age often ignore or don't pay any attention to? (Younger children. Kids they don't like.)

3. What are some things you could do to care for someone who doesn't seem to have any friends?

Additional Information for Older Children

Elizabeth Fry made sure the women prisoners were given Bibles and other things they needed. Many of her ideas for helping women who were in prison became laws in England and other countries. Elizabeth became very famous for her good works. In addition to helping women in prisons, Elizabeth taught children to read in Sunday School, helped start libraries and even started a school to train nurses in caring for people.

Running the Race

Teacher's Materials

Bible with bookmark at Acts 5:29, sports medal or trophy.

Introduce the Object Talk

We show goodness by choosing to obey God. Let's find out about one man who chose to obey God, even when it was hard.

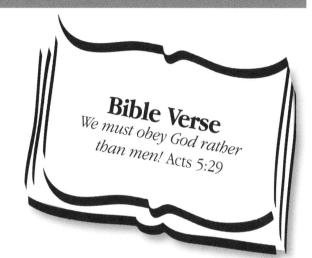

Bible Verse
We must obey God rather than men! Acts 5:29

Present the Object Talk

1. Show sports medal or trophy. **How do you think I got this award?** Volunteers tell ideas. Briefly explain to children where the item came from. **Many athletes dream of the chance to win Olympic medals.**

2. Eric Liddell (lih-DEHL) was an athlete in England who could run very fast! In 1924, he hoped to win a gold medal at the Olympics. But when the race schedules were announced, Eric discovered that he was supposed to run in a race on a Sunday. Years before, Eric had said that he would not work or play sports on Sundays. He made this choice to show his love and obedience to God. Eric wanted to spend time worshiping God on Sundays, not running races. So Eric said he would not run in the Sunday race.

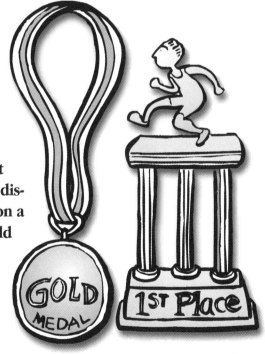

When people in England heard about Eric's decision, they were furious! They thought that Eric didn't care about his country. But Eric started training for a different race that did not take place on Sunday. No one thought he could win this race, however, because it was longer. On the day of the race, much to everyone's surprise, Eric not only won the race and the gold medal, but he also ran this race faster than anyone else in the world had ever run it!

Conclude

Read Acts 5:29 aloud. **How did Eric Liddell show that he wanted to obey God? Why might it have been hard for him to show goodness in this way?** Children respond. Pray, asking God to help children choose to obey Him, even when it is hard.

Bible Verse
We must obey God rather than men! Acts 5:29

Discussion Questions

1. How do we know what God wants us to do? (He tells us in His Word, the Bible. By listening to our parents.) **What are some things God's Word tells us to do?** Volunteers respond. Invite older children to read one or more of the following verses aloud: Exodus 20:12, Galatians 5:14, 1 Thessalonians 5:16-18, James 1:19, 1 John 3:11.

2. Why is it most important to obey God? (His laws are the best, even when they are hard. He loves us. He is God, the maker of everything. His laws tell us how to follow God's plans.)

3. When are some times it is hard to obey God's commands? (When you feel tired or angry. When you don't know God's commands. When everyone else is disobeying God's commands.) **Why do you think it's important to obey God, even in those hard times?**

4. Name one way you can show goodness by obeying God's commands this week.

Additional Information for Older Children

Throughout his life, Eric Liddell made choices that showed goodness. Just one year after winning the Olympic gold medal, Eric went to the country of China as a missionary. For 20 years, Eric Liddell helped people in China learn about Jesus. The story of Eric Liddell's life and his good choices was told in the movie *Chariots of Fire.*

Care for Foster Children

Sharing what you have can show your love for God and bring kindness to many people.

Teacher's Materials
Bible with bookmark at Romans 12:13, food wrapper or bag from a fast-food restaurant.

Introduce the Object Talk
We can bring kindness to many people when we share what we have. As we learn about one person who shared, think about how you can show God's love by sharing and bringing kindness to others.

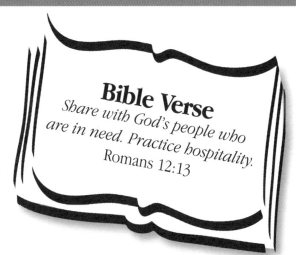

Bible Verse
Share with God's people who are in need. Practice hospitality.
Romans 12:13

Present the Object Talk
1. Show food wrapper or bag. **What do you know about the place where I got this (wrapper)?** Children respond. **S. Truett Cathy is one person who started a fast-food restaurant.**

2. When he was a young man, Truett Cathy had a dream of owning a restaurant. He worked hard and saved his money. In 1946, Truett and his brother opened their first restaurant. Eventually, Truett started a chain of fast-food restaurants called Chick-fil-A. Chick-fil-A restaurants became very popular and soon Truett was rich.

Some rich people spend their money on big houses or new cars. But Truett loved God and believed the Bible verse that says that it is better "to give than to receive" (Acts 20:35). Truett chose to spend his money helping children in foster care— children who have to live away from their parents, because their parents can't take good care of them.

Many times children in foster care don't even get to keep living with their brothers and sisters. Truett felt sorry for these children, so he used his money to build foster homes where brothers and sisters could live together. Foster parents also live in

the homes, so the children have a safe place to live and grow. Foster children in these homes are loved and cared for.

Conclude

Bible Verse
Share with God's people who are in need. Practice hospitality.
Romans 12:13

Read Romans 12:13 aloud. **How did Truett Cathy obey this verse? How do you think his actions made a difference in other people's lives?** Children tell ideas. **It pleases God when the members of His family are kind and share what they have with others.** Lead children in prayer, asking for God's help to find opportunities to be kind and share with others. Talk with interested children about becoming members of God's family (refer to "Leading a Child to Christ" article on p. 12).

Discussion Questions

1. **What do you think are some good reasons for obeying Romans 12:13?** (To show God's love. To show that we thank God for His love.)

2. **What are some things needed by people you know?**

3. **What can you share with others?** (Clothes. Friendship. Knowledge of God's love.)

Additional Information for Older Children

In addition to sharing money to help foster children, Truett Cathy gave money to Chick-fil-A workers who wanted to go to college. Since 1973, the company has given more than $15 million to help their workers go to college.

Fair Pay for All

Teacher's Materials

Bible with bookmark at Romans 12:18, Help Wanted section of newspaper.

Introduce the Object Talk

Every day we have opportunities to help others live in peace. Peacemakers do what they can to put the needs and interests of others first. Let's find out what one man did to be a peacemaker.

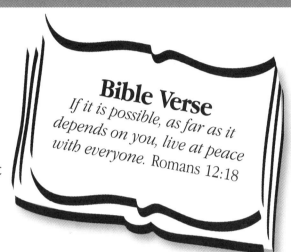

Bible Verse
If it is possible, as far as it depends on you, live at peace with everyone. Romans 12:18

Present the Object Talk

1. Show Help Wanted section of newspaper. **What do people use this part of the newspaper for? Why might finding a job be hard?** Children tell ideas. **There are all kinds of reasons people might have a hard time finding jobs. Some people have had trouble finding good jobs just because of the color of their skin.**

2. John Perkins was an African-American who had a hard time finding a job for fair pay. He once worked for a farmer all day and received only 15 cents as payment! Because of problems like these, many African-American people believed they needed to fight to be treated fairly.

3. When John Perkins grew up, he became a Christian. He wanted to help African-Americans be treated fairly without fighting. So John started telling people in Mississippi about Jesus. Sometimes he was yelled at and even beaten, but he still worked hard to help African-Americans get fair pay.

One time a friend of John's told him about a man and woman who were so poor that they didn't have any food or a place to live. John said he would help the man and woman. When they came for help, however, John was surprised to see that they were not African-American! John wondered if he should help them or not. But he soon realized that because God loves everyone the same, white people deserved help from him, too. John's hard work helped people of all races get good jobs and fair pay.

Bible Verse

If it is possible, as far as it depends on you, live at peace with everyone. Romans 12:18

Conclude

Read Romans 12:18 aloud. **What does the verse mean when it says we should live at peace with others "as far as it depends on [us]"?** (It means we should not start fights or arguments. It means we should try to end arguments or fights, instead of continuing them.) **In what ways was John Perkins a peacemaker?** (He helped others to get good jobs and fair pay without fighting.) Lead children in prayer, asking God to help them do what they can this week to live at peace with others.

Discussion Questions

1. When might a kid your age need help to live in peace with others? (When someone says something mean. When someone cheats in a game.)

2. Who are some peacemakers you know? (Police officers. People who break up fights. People who walk away from arguments.)

3. What can you do to make peace if someone wants to quarrel? (Stop a quarrel instead of continuing it. Ask an adult for help. Pray, asking God for courage to be a peacemaker.)

Additional Information for Older Children

John Perkins started the Harambee (HAR-ahm-bay) Christian Family Center in Pasadena, California. The word "Harambee" is Swahili and means "let's pull together." The people who work at this center help teenagers go to college, so they can come back to help others.

A Dangerous Journey

We can ask God for wisdom to settle arguments and live in peace with others.

Teacher's Materials

Bible with bookmark at Romans 14:19, sheriff's badge; optional—construction paper, marker, scissors, straight pin.

Prepare the Activity

(Optional: Make badge from construction paper [see sketch].)

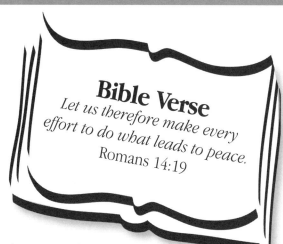

Bible Verse

Let us therefore make every effort to do what leads to peace.
Romans 14:19

Introduce the Object Talk

God will help us live in peace with others when we ask Him for help and wisdom to settle arguments. Let's find out about a man who had to be very brave to live in peace.

Present the Object Talk

1. Invite a volunteer to wear sheriff's badge. (Optional: Volunteer wears paper badge.) **What is the job of someone who wears a badge like this?** (Sheriff. Police officer.) **How does a sheriff or police officer keep the peace?**

2. In the 1800s a young man named Samuel Morris had a chance to help others live in peace. Samuel was sailing on a ship from the African country of Liberia to America, because he wanted to go to school to learn more about God.

The sailors on the ship, however, didn't like Samuel because he was African. One angry sailor even threatened to kill him! One day, that sailor thought others were making fun of him, so he swung his sword to attack them. Samuel jumped in the way, putting his own life in danger, and shouted, "Don't kill!" The angry sailor surprised everyone by putting down his sword and walking away. Everyone was amazed! After that, whenever there was a fight, Samuel helped to stop it and kept the peace by praying for the men. Samuel Morris showed that he was willing to do whatever he could to help people live peacefully together.

Conclude

Read Romans 14:19 aloud. **What does it mean to "make every effort"?** (To try as hard as you can. To do something to the best of your ability.) **How did Samuel Morris show that he made every effort for peace?** (Even though he could have been hurt or killed, he stopped the sailor with the sword from hurting anyone.) Invite volunteers to pray, asking God to help them do actions that will help friends and family members live in peace.

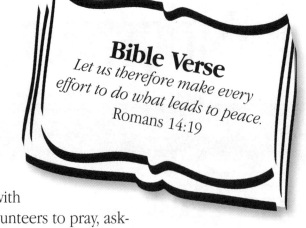

Bible Verse

Let us therefore make every effort to do what leads to peace.
Romans 14:19

Discussion Questions

1. When have you been a peacemaker or settled an argument while playing with friends? With your family? Tell children an age-appropriate example about God giving you wisdom to be a peacemaker before asking children to share their stories.

2. When is one of the hardest times for you to remember to be a peacemaker?

3. How can you make every effort to do what leads to peace at home? At school? (Let a brother or sister be first or borrow something when he or she asks. Ask God for wisdom about how to treat a classmate who is being mean. Don't argue. Don't tease.)

Additional Information for Older Children

Samuel Morris was born a prince in Africa. When he was a teenager, he was taken prisoner when his people lost a battle. Samuel was tortured when his father could not pay the ransom. After sailing to America, Samuel attended Taylor University in America for only one year before he died from injuries he had received when he was tortured. But during that year, Samuel helped many people learn to trust and obey God. Many people at Taylor University decided to become missionaries because of Samuel's actions.

In Sickness and in Health

Because Jesus loves and accepts us, we can show His love to all kinds of people.

Teacher's Materials

Bible with bookmark at Romans 15:7, one or more Hawaiian items (lei, shirt, pictures of Hawaii, etc.).

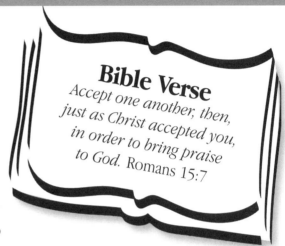

Bible Verse
Accept one another, then, just as Christ accepted you, in order to bring praise to God. Romans 15:7

Introduce the Object Talk

Because of Jesus' love for and acceptance of us, we can show His love to other people, no matter who they are or where they live. Let's find out about some people who were difficult to accept and care for.

Present the Object Talk

1. Show Hawaiian item(s). **What do you think of when you hear someone talk about Hawaii?** Children tell ideas. **We usually think that because Hawaii is so beautiful, everyone who lives there must be happy! But a long time ago, in the 1800s, there were some people living in Hawaii who weren't happy because they were sick with leprosy (a disease now called Hansen's disease).**

2. At that time there was no treatment for leprosy, so everyone in Hawaii with leprosy was sent away to live on the Hawaiian island of Molokai (MOH-loh-ki). Ships came to bring food and medicine, but no healthy person lived on Molokai to help the sick people living there.

Then a man named Father Damien heard about the people who were sick with leprosy. Even though Father Damien lived far away from Hawaii in the country of Belgium and even though he knew that he could get sick, too, he moved to Molokai.

Father Damien was a friend to the people with leprosy. He taught them to grow crops and take better care of themselves. He gave the people medicine and helped them bandage their sores. Father Damien stayed with the people he cared about until he got sick and died from leprosy himself.

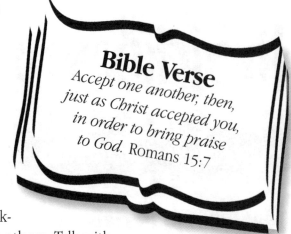

Bible Verse
Accept one another, then, just as Christ accepted you, in order to bring praise to God. Romans 15:7

Conclude

Read Romans 15:7 aloud. **How did Father Damien show that he accepted others?** Volunteers respond. **God showed His care for us by sending Jesus so that we can become members of God's family.** Pray, asking God to help children accept and care for others. Talk with interested children about becoming members of God's family (refer to "Leading a Child to Christ" article on p. 12).

Discussion Questions

1. When are some times that it is hard to accept others or treat them like friends?

2. What are some good reasons to accept others? (Christ accepts us and loves us.)

3. How can you show friendship and acceptance this week to someone who hasn't been a friend before?

Additional Information for Older Children

Father Damien's love and acceptance of the lepers in Hawaii helped them live better lives and even caused people in other countries to help people with leprosy. In 1889, when Father Damien died from leprosy, the news of his death spread quickly around the world. Many people started working harder than ever before to find a cure for leprosy. Today, taking medicines can cure most people who become sick with leprosy.

Have a Seat!

Teacher's Materials

Bible with bookmark at 1 Corinthians 13:7, newspaper.

Introduce the Object Talk

God shows patience by forgiving us and loving us, even when we don't deserve it. When we realize God's patience with us, it helps us be patient with others. Let's find out how some people showed patience.

Bible Verse

[Love] always protects, always trusts, always hopes, always perseveres. 1 Corinthians 13:7

Present the Object Talk

1. Give each child a sheet of newspaper. **What can you do with a newspaper?** Children demonstrate ideas. **In China, some people used newspapers in an unusual way.**

2. Pastor Li was the leader of a church in China that met in a house. It was against the law for this church to meet and for Pastor Li to preach about Jesus. But he didn't stop. Because of his preaching, Pastor Li was arrested and severely beaten many times.

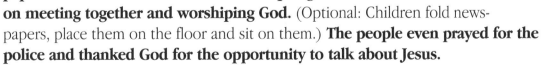

One day the police came to the church meeting and not only took every Bible they found, but they also took all the chairs! Still, the people didn't give up meeting together. They patiently folded up newspapers to sit on instead of chairs and kept right on meeting together and worshiping God. (Optional: Children fold newspapers, place them on the floor and sit on them.) **The people even prayed for the police and thanked God for the opportunity to talk about Jesus.**

Conclude

Read 1 Corinthians 13:7 aloud. **What word in this verse means the same thing as "patient"?** ("Perseveres.") **To persevere means to keep on doing something, even** when it's hard. When we remember God's patience toward us, it helps us keep on showing patience to others. **How did Pastor Li and the people in his church show patience?** (They kept on worshiping God and praying for others, even when the police made it hard.) Pray, thanking God for His patience and asking His help in showing patience toward others.

Bible Verse

[Love] always protects, always trusts, always hopes, always perseveres. 1 Corinthians 13:7

Discussion Questions

1. How does God show patience toward us? (He forgives us when we're sorry. He takes care of us, even when we don't thank Him.)

2. When is a time you need to keep on showing patience toward others? (When others make fun of me. When others don't keep their promises.)

3. What are some ways you could show patience with others? (Not yelling back when someone starts yelling. Waiting to take a turn without complaining. Praying every day for a friend who is sick, even if he or she doesn't get well right away.)

4. What can help you show patience when it's hard? (Remembering God's love for me.)

Additional Information for Older Children

One night as Pastor Li was preaching, the police came and arrested him. Instead of fighting with them, Pastor Li and his people simply prayed for the police. As the police took Pastor Li to their car, they noticed he was carrying a bag with him. They asked him what was in the bag. Pastor Li explained that the bag had a blanket and some clothes in it. Three years earlier, the police had threatened to arrest him, so Pastor Li had packed a bag that he kept for three years in case the police came back to arrest him.

Making Friends

Teacher's Materials

Bible with bookmark at 1 Corinthians 15:58, bucket, rope, small prize for each child.

Prepare the Activity

Tie rope onto bucket's handle. Place prizes in bucket.

Introduce the Object Talk

Doing what's right, even in difficult situations, is a way to show patience. Let's find out how a man showed patience in a hard situation.

Bible Verse
Stand firm. Let nothing move you. Always give yourselves fully to the work of the Lord.
1 Corinthians 15:58

Present the Object Talk

1. What kind of gift would you give a friend? Volunteers respond. **I'm going to give you a gift in an unusual way today.** Hold bucket by the rope and invite each child to take a prize from the bucket. **Usually when people exchange gifts, it shows that they are friends. Let's find out how a man named Jim Elliot gave gifts in a bucket to try to make friends with some dangerous people.**

2. Jim Elliot and four other missionaries lived in the country of Ecuador in South America. The missionaries wanted to tell a group of people called the Aucas (OW-kuhs) about Jesus. But there was a BIG problem. The Aucas were not friendly people. In fact, they usually killed anyone who came near their villages!

But the missionaries didn't give up. First, they patiently learned how to say words in the Aucan language. Then for several months, they flew over the Aucas' villages, lowering buckets filled with gifts for the Aucas. As they lowered the buckets, they called out greetings to the people. Even in this hard situation, Jim Elliot patiently kept trying to make friends with the Aucas. Eventually, the missionaries were able to meet the Aucas face-to-face.

Conclude

Read 1 Corinthians 15:58. **"Stand firm"** **means you should keep doing what is right and trust in God. What is one way Jim Elliot and his friends stood firm and did the work of the Lord?** (They continued to try to make friends with the Aucas, even though it was hard.) Pray, asking God to help children patiently do what is right.

Bible Verse

Stand firm. Let nothing move you. Always give yourselves fully to the work of the Lord.
1 Corinthians 15:58

Discussion Questions

1. What are some situations in which it is hard to have patience and do what is right? (Your brother or sister keeps bothering you. Someone is yelling at you. You are tired and don't want to do what is right.)

2. What is one right action you can take (when your younger brother keeps taking your markers)? Repeat question, substituting other situations in which patience might be needed.

3. What is "the work of the Lord"? (Loving others. Obeying God's commands.)

4. Name one time (at school) when it is hard to do what is right. How can you patiently keep doing right in that situation? Repeat question, substituting other times, places or situations for the words "at school."

Additional Information for Older Children

Shortly after Jim Elliot and his friends met the Aucas, they were killed by the Aucas. Some people thought that all of Jim's efforts to make friends had been wasted. But several years later, Jim's wife and another woman became friends with the Aucas and lived in their village. Because the missionaries patiently kept doing what was right, many Aucas became Christians.

Choosing Self-Control

Depending on God for self-control helps us make good choices.

Teacher's Materials
Bible with bookmark at 1 Corinthians 16:13, one or more ears of corn (if possible, bring corn still in its husk).

Introduce the Object Talk
Asking God for help with self-control can help us make good choices. Let's find out about someone who depended on God's help and made good choices.

Bible Verse
Be on your guard; stand firm in the faith; be men of courage; be strong. 1 Corinthians 16:13

Present the Object Talk
1. Show ear(s) of corn. **We usually eat the corn and throw the husk and the cob away. One man, Peter Cartwright, used an entire cornstalk to show self-control and to help another person do the same thing.**

2. In the early part of the 1800s, many families in America lived far away from each other. One of the few times these families would get together was when a traveling preacher, like Peter Cartwright, came to visit. Each time Peter came to an area where several families lived, he led church meetings and talked with the families about God.

After one of these church meetings, Peter was invited to dinner at a nearby home. One of the men at the dinner was angry with Peter, because he thought that Peter had treated the man's son unfairly. The man challenged Peter to a duel to the death!

Peter could have gotten angry with the man. Instead he just said, "According to the rules of honor, I have the right to choose the weapon. Isn't that right?" The man nodded. Peter smiled and said, "Let's go outside and grab a couple of cornstalks to fight with. I think that ought to settle things. Don't you?" The other man started to laugh and realized that he didn't need to be so angry. Soon the argument ended. At the next church meeting, the man became a member of God's family.

Conclude

Read 1 Corinthians 16:13 aloud. **How did Peter Cartwright obey this verse?** (Peter didn't get angry. He helped the other man do what was right.) **How did his self-control help to avoid trouble?** Children respond. Lead children in prayer, asking for God's help to have self-control and make good choices. **One good choice we can all make is to become members of God's family.** Talk with interested children about becoming members of God's family (see "Leading a Child to Christ" on p. 12).

Bible Verse
Be on your guard; stand firm in the faith; be men of courage; be strong. 1 Corinthians 16:13

Discussion Questions

1. When do you think a kid your age needs self-control?

2. When were some times you needed to have self-control? How did your self-control help the situation? What might have happened if you didn't have self-control?

3. What can you do when you need self-control and the ability to make good choices? (Pray to God and ask for His help. Remember Bible verses that tell about God's help.)

Additional Information for Older Children

Peter Cartwright hated slavery and in 1824, he moved his family to the state of Illinois. In Illinois, it was against the law to own slaves. Peter Cartwright decided to become a government leader and won many elections. His only defeat was in 1846 when he lost an election for the Unites States Congress to Abraham Lincoln! Peter Cartwright wrote the story of his life in the book *Autobiography of Peter Cartwright, The Backwoods Preacher*.

Service with a Smile

Be ready to serve others with a gentle attitude.

Teacher's Materials
Bible with bookmark at Galatians 5:13, scrub brush, bucket.

Introduce the Object Talk
Being ready to serve others with a gentle attitude helps us show God's love. Let's find out how someone showed God's love with a scrub brush.

Bible Verse
Serve one another in love.
Galatians 5:13

Present the Object Talk
1. Show scrub brush and bucket. **When have you used a scrub brush or bucket?** Volunteers tell. **Some people don't like to wash floors or cars, because they think it's not very important work. In 1895 a woman named Amy Carmichael had to scrub something dirty to show what it meant to serve others.**

2. Amy had gone to India as a missionary. She noticed that many children needed a safe place to live. Some of these children came to live with Amy. Soon Amy was taking care of 17 children! Sometimes Amy wondered if she had been right in giving up important work in other places to take care of the children. But Amy remembered that Jesus showed God's love by serving His disciples and washing their feet. Taking care of the children was valuable, because it was a way she could serve others and show God's love!

3. One day a new woman came to help care for the children. Amy asked the woman to serve by washing the nursery floor. The woman refused, because she wanted an easier, better job. So Amy took the bucket of soapy water and got down on her hands and knees and scrubbed the dirty floor. Because Amy was willing to do this hard work, she gently helped the woman learn how important it is to show God's love by serving others in whatever way is needed.

Conclude

Read Galatians 5:13 aloud. **What are some ways Amy Carmichael served others with love?** Children respond. **Let's ask God to help us serve others with gentle attitudes.** Lead children in prayer.

Bible Verse
Serve one another in love.
Galatians 5:13

Discussion Questions

1. What do you think the verse means when it says to "serve" someone with love?
(Be kind and gentle when we help. Don't have a bossy or proud attitude. Pay attention to the needs of others.)

2. What are some ways to serve others? (Get a glass of water for someone who is sitting down resting. Set the table without being asked. Help your mom by taking care of younger brothers or sisters while she cooks dinner. Make a card for someone who is sick.)

3. What can you do this week to serve others at school? At home? On the playground?

Additional Information for Older Children

Amy Carmichael broke her leg when she was older. Her leg didn't heal correctly, so she couldn't walk for the rest of her life. Instead of being angry that she couldn't do the things she had done before, Amy still served others by writing many books that helped people learn more about missionaries and about God's love for people all over the world.

God's Smuggler

Growing the fruit of the Spirit in our lives begins when we believe Jesus is God's Son, ask forgiveness for our sins and become part of God's family.

Teacher's Materials

Bible with bookmark at Galatians 5:22,23; suitcase packed with clothes and several Bibles; optional—hide Bibles in room.

Introduce the Object Talk

When we're growing God's good fruit in our lives, we show that we are members of God's family by the things we do. Let's find out how someone showed love for God.

Bible Verse

The fruit of the Spirit is love, joy, peace, patience, kindness, goodness, faithfulness, gentleness and self-control. Against such things there is no law. Galatians 5:22,23

Present the Object Talk

1. A man called Brother Andrew didn't grow up loving God. In fact, when he was a young man, he loved doing dangerous things and didn't care if other people got hurt because of his actions.

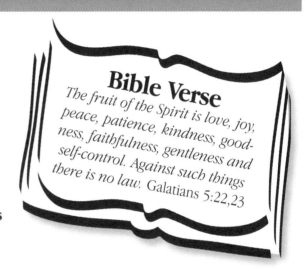

But one day Brother Andrew began to read the Bible and realized that God loved him and forgave him for his wrong actions. His love for God and others began to grow. As he learned more about loving God, Brother Andrew worked hard to show love to other people and find ways to tell them about Jesus.

2. Show suitcase. **What do you think is in this suitcase?** Invite a volunteer to look through suitcase to find Bibles. (Optional: Children find Bibles hidden in room.) **Brother Andrew heard of some countries where the government did not allow Bibles. So he hid Bibles in his suitcases and car and took them to Christians in these countries. If the hidden Bibles had been discovered, Brother Andrew could have been put in jail. God helped Brother Andrew, and he was able to safely deliver many, many Bibles. The actions of Brother Andrew showed how much he loved God and how much he wanted others to love God.**

Conclude

Read Galatians 5:22,23 aloud. **These verses tell us the good ways in which God's Holy Spirit helps each member of His family live. Which of these characteristics have you seen someone show? How?** Children respond. **Which of these characteristics did Brother Andrew show?** (Love. Kindness. Faithfulness.) Pray, asking God to help children show love for God in their actions and words. Talk with interested children about becoming members of God's family (see "Leading a Child to Christ" on p. 12).

Bible Verse

The fruit of the Spirit is love, joy, peace, patience, kindness, goodness, faithfulness, gentleness and self-control. Against such things there is no law. Galatians 5:22,23

Discussion Questions

1. Which of the fruit of the Spirit in Galatians 5:22,23 are hardest for kids your age to show?

2. When might a kid your age show love? Patience? Joy? Repeat with other fruit of the Spirit, as time allows.

3. How can others know that we are part of God's family and that we love Him? (We can tell others about our love for God. They can see the fruit of the Spirit in our lives.)

Additional Information for Older Children

The name Brother Andrew was like a nickname. Because some countries didn't want Brother Andrew to bring Bibles to their people, he didn't want everyone to know his real name. Another nickname Brother Andrew had was "God's Smuggler." *God's Smuggler* was also the name of a book that Brother Andrew wrote about the exciting ways that God helped him show love to others.

Job Training ✓ Oct/03.

Show faithfulness by doing what God wants you to do.

Teacher's Materials
Bible with bookmark at Galatians 6:9, table-cloth, place setting (plate, utensils, glass or cup).

Introduce the Object Talk
When we do what God wants us to, we show faithfulness to God. Let's find out about a woman who helped others learn to show faithfulness.

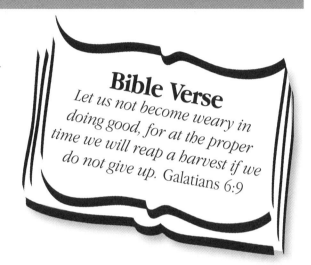

Bible Verse
Let us not become weary in doing good, for at the proper time we will reap a harvest if we do not give up. Galatians 6:9

Present the Object Talk
1. Invite volunteers to use items you brought to show how to set a table. **For what kinds of jobs would you need to know how to set a table?** (Waiter.) **What are some other jobs you know of?** Volunteers answer. **In the early 1900s many African-Americans had a hard time finding good jobs. Mary McLeod Bethune was an African-American schoolteacher who wanted her students to be able to get good jobs.**

2. Mary started a school for African-American children. She taught her students how to read, how to study Bible stories and how to speak a language called Latin. She also taught practical skills like setting tables, cooking, gardening, sewing and cleaning. Mary wanted her students to have a good education, and she wanted them to have practical skills so that they could get good jobs.

One day some of the students had to wash white linen tablecloths. Mary told the girls to boil the tablecloths to get the tablecloths clean. But the girls didn't want to make a fire and wait for the water in the large kettle to boil before they could finish the job! Not much later, Mary saw the girls hanging up the tablecloths to dry. When Mary asked if the girls had boiled the tablecloths, they admitted that they had not. Mary insisted that the girls do the job again—the right way. Mary wanted her students to understand that being faithful and not giving up was important in every job they did, even washing tablecloths.

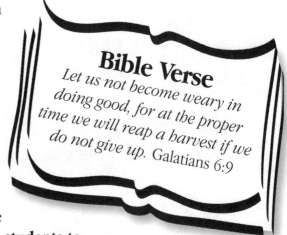

Bible Verse

Let us not become weary in doing good, for at the proper time we will reap a harvest if we do not give up. Galatians 6:9

Conclude

Read Galatians 6:9 aloud. **When might kids today show faithfulness?** (Caring for a younger brother or sister. Doing a chore without being reminded.) **What is an example of a way Mary McLeod Bethune taught her students to show faithfulness?** (She made them boil the tablecloths in order to do a good job.) **Let's ask God to help us show faithfulness by doing what He wants.** Lead children in prayer.

Discussion Questions

1. **What does it mean to be faithful?** (To do what God wants consistently.)

2. **What are some things that God wants us to do faithfully?** (Be fair. Tell the truth.)

3. Read Galatians 6:9. **When might kids your age get tired, or grow weary, of obeying God?**

Additional Information for Older Children

Mary McLeod Bethune not only taught others to show faithfulness, but she also showed faithfulness to God herself! Mary attended Moody Bible Institute in Chicago and hoped to become a missionary to Africa. When she wasn't able to do that, she decided to stay in the United States and start a school for African-American children. The small school she started with five students in 1904 is now Bethune-Cookman College in Daytona, Florida. Because of Mary's faithfulness, thousands of students still learn about God each year!

A Chance to Learn

Don't miss an opportunity to show goodness by doing what is right.

Teacher's Materials

Bible with bookmark at Galatians 6:10, item typically given to a teacher as a gift (bell; apple; sign saying "Thank you, teacher!"; etc.).

Bible Verse
As we have opportunity, let us do good to all people, especially to those who belong to the family of believers. Galatians 6:10

Introduce the Object Talk

We should use every chance we have to show goodness by doing what is right. Let's find out about someone who showed goodness and helped others because she did what was right.

Present the Object Talk

1. Hold up teacher gift. **Have you ever given something like this to one of your teachers or seen anything like this on one of your teachers' desks? What other kinds of gifts might make a teacher feel special?** Volunteers respond. **A long time ago, a teacher named Prudence Crandall got the opposite of a thank-you gift from the people who lived around her school.**

Teachers change the world one child at a time!

2. In the early 1800s, when people were still fighting about slavery, Prudence Crandall started a school for teenage girls in Connecticut. All the girls attending the school were white. At that time, some people did not want to be friends with African-Americans. So when Prudence welcomed an African-American girl to attend the school, people in her town got angry. They took their daughters out of the school. But Prudence loved all of God's people and wanted to give African-American students a chance to learn. She invited more African-American girls to the school to take the place of the students who had left.

Now the townspeople became very upset! When a group of angry townspeople attacked her school, Prudence closed the school because she was afraid the girls would get hurt. It seemed like anger and hatred had won. But when some of her students grew up, they helped other African-American girls get an education. The good choices Prudence Crandall made caused many people to be able to learn. That was even better than receiving a thank-you gift!

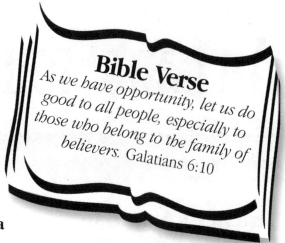

Bible Verse
As we have opportunity, let us do good to all people, especially to those who belong to the family of believers. Galatians 6:10

Conclude

Read Galatians 6:10 aloud. **What does this verse tell us to do for all people? How did Prudence Crandall do good for others?** (She tried to help young girls by teaching them, even though other people didn't want her to.) Close in prayer, thanking God for the opportunity to do good and asking for His help in choosing to do what is right.

Discussion Questions

1. When might a kid your age be able to show goodness by choosing to do what is right? (Choosing to say something nice to a kid who is being teased. Let your brother or sister have the first turn, instead of fighting about whose turn it is.)

2. When has someone shown goodness to you by doing what was right? How did that make you feel? Tell your own answer as well as asking volunteers to respond.

3. What are some ways to learn the right things to do? (Read the Bible. Listen to parents or teachers. Watch older people who love Jesus.)

Additional Information for Older Children

Prudence Crandall was arrested and put on trial because of her efforts to help young African-American girls. Even though Prudence was found guilty and had to spend time in jail, her trial ended up helping others. More than 100 years later, some of the things said at her trial were used in the Supreme Court of the United States to make new laws that help African-Americans get good educations.

An Itchy Situation

God's gift of joy can help us be thankful in any situation.

Teacher's Materials

Bible with bookmark at Ephesians 5:19,20; anti-itch cream or lotion; optional—cotton swabs.

Introduce the Object Talk

We can be thankful in any situation, because of the joy God gives to us. Let's find out about an unusual situation in which two women found that they could be thankful.

Bible Verse
Sing and make music in your heart to the Lord, always giving thanks to God the Father for everything, in the name of our Lord Jesus Christ.
Ephesians 5:19,20

Present the Object Talk

1. Show anti-itch cream or lotion. (Optional: Use cotton swabs to dab a small amount of cream or lotion on hands of volunteers.) **When might someone need an anti-itch (lotion)?** Children respond. **Many years ago, during World War II, a woman named Corrie ten Boom and her sister, Betsy, could have used a (lotion) like this.**

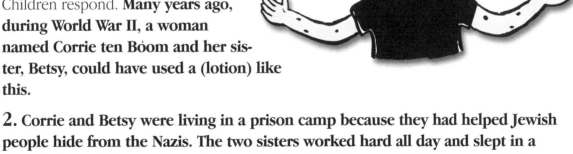

2. Corrie and Betsy were living in a prison camp because they had helped Jewish people hide from the Nazis. The two sisters worked hard all day and slept in a crowded, smelly room at night. Corrie often felt like complaining—especially because the room in which they slept was full of fleas. Fleas hopped everywhere. They even lived in the straw that the women had to sleep on. The itching was awful. Things seemed terrible!

Betsy reminded Corrie that God could do good things in any situation. They thanked Him for the fleas. But they must have wondered how God could make something good happen in their terrible situation.

Each night Corrie and Betsy read the Bible aloud to the other women in the room. At first, they posted lookouts to keep watch for the guards because anyone caught with a Bible would certainly be killed! But one day they found out that no guards ever came to their room—because of all the fleas! Corrie and Betsy thanked God because the fleas made it easier to read the Bible and teach others about God's love.

Bible Verse

Sing and make music in your heart to the Lord, always giving thanks to God the Father for everything, in the name of our Lord Jesus Christ.
Ephesians 5:19,20

Conclude

Read Ephesians 5:19,20 aloud. **What do these verses say about thanking God? Why do you think Corrie and Betsy ten Boom were able to thank God, even in a very bad situation?** (Because they knew God would always be with them and help them.) **God gives us good things and loves us, even when we are having hard times.** Invite children to pray, telling God things they are thankful for.

Discussion Questions

1. **When are some times that it is hard to thank God? Why?**

2. **What could you give thanks for when you have a bad day at school?** (You can read. You have a school to attend.) **When you are sick?** (You have a bed to rest in.)

3. **What are some ways to show God's gift of joy?** (Singing or playing an instrument in a song of praise. Telling others about God.)

Additional Information for Older Children

Corrie, Betsy and the other members of their family were arrested by the Nazis for hiding Jewish people in their home. On the top floor of their house, a small secret room was built behind Corrie's bedroom. In that tiny room, they hid Jewish people. Even though all of Corrie and Betsy's family were arrested, none of the Jewish people they hid were ever found. After World War II ended, Corrie wrote many books. One book, *The Hiding Place*, is about her family's adventures hiding Jewish people from the Nazis.

A School for Girls

Teacher's Materials

Bible with bookmark at Ephesians 6:7, long strips of cloth or an elastic bandage.

Introduce the Object Talk

We can use our abilities to show kindness to other people. Let's find out how one woman's actions helped others learn to be kind.

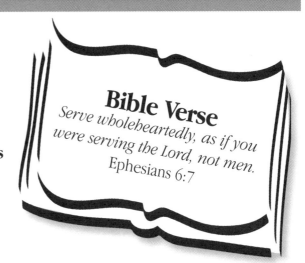

Bible Verse
Serve wholeheartedly, as if you were serving the Lord, not men.
Ephesians 6:7

Present the Object Talk

1. Invite a volunteer to wrap his or her arm or ankle in cloths or bandage. **When are some times people wrap their arms or ankles like this?** (When they've sprained or broken their arm or ankle.) **A long time ago in China, people wrapped the feet of girls for a very different reason. At that time in China, people thought that small feet were beautiful! Parents tightly wrapped their daughters' feet with the small toes bent under. The bones in the feet would break and then heal into tiny twisted feet that were very painful to walk on.**

2. In 1873, a woman named Lottie Moon went to China as a missionary. She wanted to help people learn about Jesus. Lottie started a school for girls. But Lottie soon found that her students had a hard time learning. The girls were in constant pain because their feet were bound so tightly!

Lottie felt so sorry for her students that she worked hard to convince one girl's family to let the girl unbind her feet. It wasn't easy for Lottie Moon to convince others to stop hurting girls by binding their feet. But in time, Lottie's actions convinced many people to treat girls kindly; and eventually, foot binding became illegal.

Conclude

Read Ephesians 6:7 aloud. **How did Lottie Moon show that she served God?** (She convinced people not to hurt girls by binding their feet.) **Lottie Moon used her ability to talk to people to help the girls in her school. Let's ask God to help us use our abilities to show kindness to others, too.** Lead children in prayer.

Bible Verse
Serve wholeheartedly, as if you were serving the Lord, not men.
Ephesians 6:7

Discussion Questions

1. What are some of the abilities God has given you? Guide children in discussing all kinds of abilities (reading well, playing soccer, being a good friend, singing, cooking, fixing things, painting, etc.).

2. What are some ways you can use these abilities to show kindness to others?

3. When has someone showed kindness to you? What ability did he or she use?

Additional Information for Older Children

During her life, Lottie Moon was very concerned that people not forget to help missionaries who teach about God in foreign countries. She wrote many letters to Christians in the United States, asking them to give money to missionaries. Lottie Moon died on Christmas Eve, 1912. To this day, in Lottie's honor, many churches still collect a Lottie Moon Christmas Offering that is used to help missionaries.

Will Work for Free

Teacher's Materials

Bible with bookmark at Philippians 2:3, money (coins and/or bills).

Introduce the Object Talk

When we have humble and gentle attitudes, we won't look down on others. Let's find out how one man showed a humble and gentle attitude.

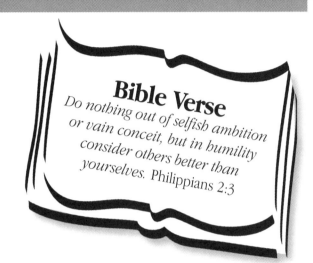

Bible Verse

Do nothing out of selfish ambition or vain conceit, but in humility consider others better than yourselves. Philippians 2:3

Present the Object Talk

1. Show money. **What are some ways people get money? Why do you think some people want to have lots of money?** Children tell ideas. **When do you think someone might NOT want to have lots of money? In the country of Japan, a man by the name of Kagawa (kah-GAH-wah) chose not to be paid a lot of money for his hard work.**

2. Kagawa lived in a shack in a poor part of his town. He lived there so that he could help the people who lived there learn about Jesus. While Kagawa was living in this part of town, a terrible earthquake destroyed most of the city. An important city leader told Kagawa that the city needed him to help people rebuild their homes, to make sure people had food to eat and water to drink and to help the poor people find good jobs. The official said, "The job pays a good salary and you will be given a car."

Kagawa surprised the official when he said that he would be glad to do the job, but he would not take money or a car. Instead, Kagawa asked that his salary be used to help poor people. Kagawa's actions showed that he was humble. He believed that the needs of poor people were just as important as his own needs.

Conclude

Read Philippians 2:3 aloud. **How did Kagawa show that he was humble?** (He lived in a small house. He asked that poor people be helped with the money he worked for.) Lead children in prayer, asking God to help children have humble and gentle attitudes.

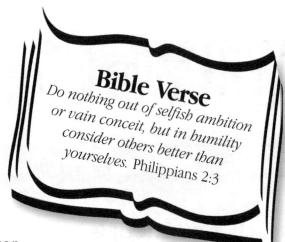

Bible Verse

Do nothing out of selfish ambition or vain conceit, but in humility consider others better than yourselves. Philippians 2:3

Discussion Questions

1. What are some ways to describe a person who is humble? (Cares about others. Remembers that other people are important. Wants to do what is best for other people.)

2. How do you feel when someone acts like he or she is better than you are? How would you want to be treated instead?

3. What are some things you could do to show a humble and gentle attitude? (Let others go first. Don't act better than everyone else. Listen carefully when others speak.)

4. When we have humble attitudes, we don't spend our time comparing ourselves to others. What should we think about instead? (Ways to love God and others. How we can help others.)

Additional Information for Older Children

A teacher, poet and scientist, Kagawa wrote 150 books. Kagawa was known to repeat three prayers: "Father, forgive"; "God, let me live to serve"; "O God, make me like Christ." These prayers showed how much Kagawa loved God and how much he wanted to obey God by helping others.

Sunday School

Show God's love by caring about the problems of others.

Teacher's Materials
Bible with bookmark at Philippians 2:4, newspaper.

Introduce the Object Talk
When we care about the problems other people have, we show God's love. Let's find out how a man who lived along ago cared about others and how he showed God's love to them.

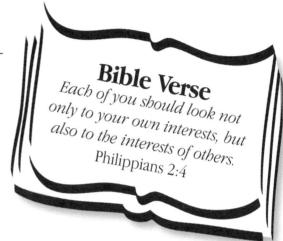

Bible Verse
Each of you should look not only to your own interests, but also to the interests of others.
Philippians 2:4

Present the Object Talk

1. Invite a volunteer to look through the newspaper to find names of people who write for the paper. **What do you think would be fun about working for a newspaper? What might be hard? Let's find out about a newspaper editor from a long time ago.**

2. Robert Raikes was born in England in 1736. Robert was the editor of a newspaper called the *Gloucester* (GLAHS-tuhr) *Journal*. But Robert was more than just a newspaper editor. He cared about the problems of the people who lived around him. Robert wrote stories in the newspaper about problems in prisons. He wanted other people to know about the problems, so they would help to make changes. Robert realized that the prisons were full of people who had grown up without learning about God's love.

Many poor children at that time didn't go to school or church. Instead they had to work from early morning to late at night in dark and dirty factories, even on Saturdays! The only day on which they didn't have to work was Sunday. Robert and a friend started a school for those children—a Sunday School. The children learned to read the Bible and heard stories about God's love. Robert wrote about the Sunday School in his newspaper. Soon churches all over the country were starting Sunday Schools to show God's love to poor children.

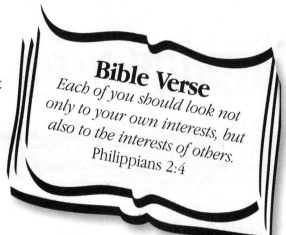

Bible Verse

Each of you should look not only to your own interests, but also to the interests of others.
Philippians 2:4

Conclude

Read Philippians 2:4 aloud. **This verse uses the word "interests" to describe problems, or things that a person worries about. How did Robert Raikes show that he cared about the worries and needs of others?** (He started a Sunday School to help children who had to work during the week.) Lead children in prayer, asking God to help them find ways to show care for other people. **God showed He cares about our needs when He sent His Son, Jesus, so that we can become members of God's family.** Talk with interested children about becoming members of God's family (refer to "Leading a Child to Christ" article on p. 12).

Discussion Questions

1. **How can you show your friends that you care about their worries and needs?**

2. **Why do you think God wants us to care about problems other people have? What might happen if we didn't care about other people's problems?**

3. **When has someone cared about a worry or need you had?**

Additional Information for Older Children

Robert Raikes wrote books for children to learn from and gave money to support these early Sunday Schools. The success of the Sunday Schools was noticed by people all over England. Robert even met King George III. After Robert Raikes died, Sunday Schools continued to grow and in 1833, the government started to pay money to support them. Eventually, Sunday Schools spread to the United States, Ireland, Scotland and all over the rest of the world!

Missionaries of Charity

Our kind actions demonstrate God's love.

Teacher's Materials

Bible with bookmark at Colossians 3:12, one or more objects with slogans (T-shirt, bumper sticker, poster, ads, etc.); optional—photo of Mother Teresa.

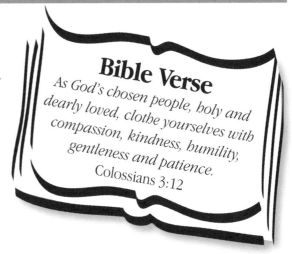

Bible Verse

As God's chosen people, holy and dearly loved, clothe yourselves with compassion, kindness, humility, gentleness and patience.
Colossians 3:12

Introduce the Object Talk

Our kind actions demonstrate God's love. Let's learn about a woman whose kind actions helped people around the world experience God's love.

Present the Object Talk

1. Show object(s) and ask volunteers to read the slogans aloud. **When people want others to know important things they believe, they often write slogans.**

2. In 1910 a special girl was born in Macedonia, a country in Eastern Europe. During her teenage years, this girl joined a group of young people who raised money for the poor and learned about missionaries in foreign lands. The motto of this group was "What have I done for Christ? What am I doing for Christ? What will I do for Christ?" This motto showed how important these teenagers thought it was to love and obey Jesus.

When this young lady was 18, she decided to serve Christ by becoming a missionary in India. For the rest of her life, she lived among the poorest people in India. She taught street children and comforted the sick and dying. She became known as Mother Teresa. Other women joined her, forming a group called the Missionaries of Charity. "Charity" is another word for "love." Today this group has more than

500 centers around the world where the hungry, the sick and the dying are cared for. (Optional: Show photo of Mother Teresa.)

Conclude

Read Colossians 3:12 aloud. **How did Mother Teresa obey this verse?** Volunteers tell. Lead children in prayer, asking for God's help serving those who are in need so that others can learn more about God's love.

Bible Verse

As God's chosen people, holy and dearly loved, clothe yourselves with compassion, kindness, humility, gentleness and patience.
Colossians 3:12

Discussion Questions

1. **What are some ways people have shown kindness to you or someone you know?**

2. **What are some kind actions you can do at home? At school? In your neighborhood?** (Let a brother or sister choose which video to watch. Help parents empty the dishwasher. Invite a new kid to play a game at school. Carry groceries for a neighbor.)

3. **Why do your kind actions help other people learn about God's love?** (They can see some of the ways God cares for them.)

4. **What is one kind action you can do this week? For whom?**

Additional Information for Older Children

The Missionaries of Charity spend their time cleaning people's bloody wounds, feeding dying people and rocking abandoned babies. When one missionary was asked if she got tired of doing this difficult work, she said that she could never get tired because she loves and cares for each person as if he or she were Jesus Himself (see Matthew 25:40).

Laundry Day

God's great love in sending Jesus to die for our sins is shown to others when we forgive them.

Teacher's Materials

Bible with bookmark at Colossians 3:13, laundry basket and/or detergent.

Introduce the Object Talk

When we have been forgiven by God, we can show His love to other people by forgiving them. Let's find out how a woman helped some people forgive each other and show God's love.

Bible Verse

Bear with each other and forgive whatever grievances you may have against one another. Forgive as the Lord forgave you. Colossians 3:13

Present the Object Talk

1. Show laundry basket and/or detergent. **What are these things used for?** Children respond. **Before washing machines had been invented, it took people many hours to wash and iron their clothes. People often hired others to do their laundry.**

2. Amanda Smith was a former slave who earned money by doing laundry for others. After her husband died, she had to work hard to earn enough money to care for her family. Amanda also worked hard so that she could spend time telling others about God's love and forgiveness.

One day after hearing Amanda speak, a young man asked for help. The man had fought with a friend several years before. Amanda's teaching helped the young man see that he needed to forgive his friend, but he was afraid to speak to him. Amanda prayed for him and said that God would help him.

The next day, the young man saw the man he had fought with. Even though he was afraid, the young man walked up to him and started to speak. The other man said, "I'm so glad you came to talk to me. I wanted to say something, but I was afraid you wouldn't speak to me!" The two men quickly forgave each other and became good friends again. Amanda felt that seeing those two men forgive each other was worth all the clothes she had to wash in order to have time to tell others about God and His love.

Bible Verse

Bear with each other and forgive whatever grievances you may have against one another. Forgive as the Lord forgave you. Colossians 3:13

Conclude

Read Colossians 3:13 aloud. **How did Amanda Smith help the two friends obey this verse?** Children respond. **Let's thank God for forgiving us and ask God to help us have courage to obey this verse and forgive others.** Lead children in prayer.

Discussion Questions

1. When have you needed to forgive a friend? What happened when you forgave your friend?

2. Why is forgiveness important? What do you think might happen to friendships if neither friend is willing to forgive the other one?

3. How does forgiveness help people get along with each other better?

Additional Information for Older Children

Amanda Smith was a friend to people all over the world! She traveled to countries all over the world to tell others about Jesus. She also started a home for orphaned African-American girls in Harvey, Illinois. The school was called the Amanda Smith Orphans Home. Amanda also wrote her autobiography, which tells about her faith in God and her missionary travels in America, England, Ireland, Scotland, India and Africa.

Love Songs

The fruit of the Spirit is shown through our love for God and others.

Teacher's Materials

Bible with bookmark at Colossians 3:14; optional—hymnal containing "Take My Life, and Let It Be" by Frances Havergal.

Introduce the Object Talk

The fruit of the Spirit is shown through our love for God and others. Let's learn how one woman showed her love for God through her whole life!

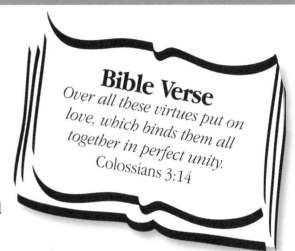

Bible Verse

Over all these virtues put on love, which binds them all together in perfect unity. Colossians 3:14

Present the Object Talk

1. Hold out your hand. **What do you use your hands to do?** Repeat question with feet and voice. **Frances Havergal is a woman who wrote a song about how she wanted to use her hands, her mouth, her money—her whole life! Frances said she wanted to use everything in her life to show her love for God and obedience to Him.** (Optional: Read the words of "Take My Life, and Let It Be" or sing the hymn together.)

2. The words that Frances wrote were not just nice-sounding words to her. She actually gave away most of her money to help others. And she often studied the Bible. In fact, Frances memorized the entire New Testament and several books in the Old Testament.

Frances spent her whole life loving God. She started writing poems about her love for God when she was only seven years old. Before she would do anything or write any songs or poems, Frances would pray. In fact, the words of "Take My Life, and Let It Be" are a prayer to God. Frances only lived to be 42 years old, but she wrote many books and poems, including over 60 songs that still help people tell about their love for God.

Conclude

Read Colossians 3:14 aloud. **What does this verse say we are to "put on," or show? How did Frances Havergal show her love for God?** (She memorized portions of the Bible. She prayed. She wrote poems and songs about God.) Lead children in prayer, expressing their love for God. (Optional: Read or sing hymn again as a prayer.) **A great way to show our love for God is to become members of His family.** Talk with interested children about becoming members of God's family (refer to "Leading a Child to Christ" article on p. 12).

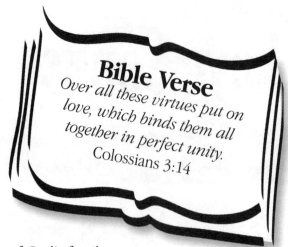

Bible Verse

Over all these virtues put on love, which binds them all together in perfect unity.
Colossians 3:14

Discussion Questions

1. How can you show love for God with your hands? Your feet? Your voice?

2. What are some actions that show love for God? (Singing songs of praise to God. Telling others about Jesus. Praying. Helping someone in need. Obeying God's commands. Giving an offering.)

3. What are some actions that show love for others? (Helping someone who is hurt. Being honest. Saying kind words.)

4. What is a way you can show love for God this week? Show love for others?

Additional Information for Older Children

One of the songs Frances wrote is "Who Is on the Lord's Side?" The title for this song is taken from Exodus 32:26 when Moses asks God's people to choose if they will love and obey God. Ask a volunteer to read the verse aloud. Then ask a volunteer to read the words of the first stanza of the song, "Who Is on the Lord's Side?" **How did Frances describe what it means to be on the Lord's side? How might kids your age show that they want to love and obey God?**

Prison Peace

Teacher's Materials
Bible with bookmark at Colossians 3:15, bell or other item used as signal for quiet (whistle, etc.).

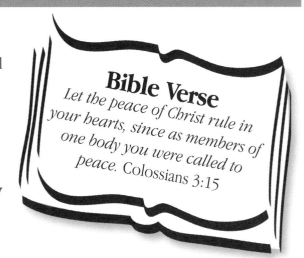

Bible Verse
Let the peace of Christ rule in your hearts, since as members of one body you were called to peace. Colossians 3:15

Introduce the Object Talk
When we do our best to make peace, it helps us make friends. Let's find out how one woman worked to make peace and what happened as a result.

Present the Object Talk
1. Get children's attention by ringing bell or using other item you brought. **If you were trying to signal a crowd of fighting people to be quiet, what would you do?** Volunteers tell. **In 1932, a woman named Gladys Aylward was asked to quiet down a crowd of fighting prisoners.**

2. Gladys Aylward had moved from England to China so that she could tell people about Jesus. "People who trust Jesus don't need to be afraid," Gladys said.

One day at a nearby prison, a fight among the prisoners was so bad that the soldiers were afraid to go into the prison to stop the fight! The governor of that area remembered what Gladys had said and asked her to make peace among the prisoners.

Gladys walked into the prison courtyard and shouted for quiet. When the men quieted down, Gladys asked them to tell her why they were fighting.

"This prison is crowded and the prisoners have nothing to do," the men said. "We fight over food because we don't have enough to eat." As Gladys talked and listened to the men, they agreed to make peace and stop fighting. Then Gladys worked hard to help keep peace among the prisoners. She even found a way for the prisoners to earn money, so they could buy enough food.

Bible Verse

Let the peace of Christ rule in your hearts, since as members of one body you were called to peace. Colossians 3:15

Conclude

Read Colossians 3:15 aloud. **When we have Christ's peace in our hearts, it means we do our best to avoid or stop fights and arguments. How did Gladys Aylward help stop fights?** (She listened to the men in the prison and helped them settle their arguments.) **Let's ask God to help us make peace with others.** Lead children in prayer.

Discussion Questions

1. When are some times kids your age have to work to make peace at school? At home? (When friends are arguing. When brothers or sisters are angry.)

2. When have you seen someone else work to make peace? What happened? Tell your own example of a situation in which working to make peace resulted in friendship.

3. When are some times people might need help to make peace? (When they are too mad to talk to each other. When they don't understand each other.)

4. How can we get God's help when we're working to make peace? (Pray to God. Read His Word. Ask older people who love God for help.)

Additional Information for Older Children

Before Gladys Aylward went to China, no one thought she would be a good missionary. But Gladys refused to give up her plan to be a missionary. She worked hard and saved money until she was able to buy a ticket to China. In China, God helped Gladys learn to speak the difficult Chinese language and to become a great missionary.

Praise the Lord

God gives us abilities and wants us to be faithful in using them.

Teacher's Materials
Bible with bookmark at Colossians 3:23, marker, paper.

Introduce the Object Talk
God gives each of us abilities that we can be faithful to use. Let's listen to find out how one woman worked hard and was faithful to use her abilities, even when it was hard.

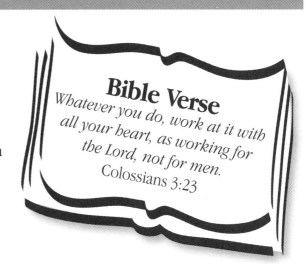

Bible Verse

Whatever you do, work at it with all your heart, as working for the Lord, not for men.
Colossians 3:23

Present the Object Talk
1. Ask a volunteer to put the marker in his or her mouth and try to draw a picture of a tree. **It's pretty hard to draw this way, but this is how a woman named Joni (JAHN-ee) Eareckson Tada learned to draw all her pictures!**

2. Joni didn't always draw this way. When Joni was a teenager, she had an accident. She dove into a lake at a place where the water was too shallow, and she broke her neck and became paralyzed. Joni could no longer use her arms or legs. But Joni was determined to be able to learn to do things again using her body parts that did work—like her mouth.

For two years, Joni worked hard to learn to draw by holding things like pencils and paintbrushes between her teeth. She began to draw beautiful pictures. Joni signed her pictures "PTL" for "Praise the Lord," reminding herself that God cared for her and thanking God for her ability to draw, even when most of her body no longer worked. Her pictures were put onto cards and sold and displayed around the world. The pictures and the "PTL" reminded people to use whatever abilities they had to give praise to God. Joni and Friends is the name of an organization

Joni started to give special encouragement to people with disabilities.

Conclude

Read Colossians 3:23 aloud. **When we are "working for the Lord," it means we are trying to do our best work to show love for God. What did Joni Eareckson Tada do to obey this verse? How did she show that she was working to please God?** (Signed her pictures "Praise the Lord.") Lead children in prayer, thanking God for the abilities He has given us.

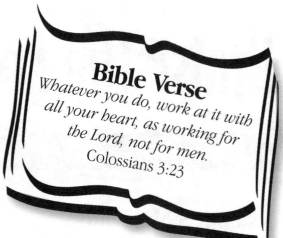

Bible Verse

Whatever you do, work at it with all your heart, as working for the Lord, not for men.
Colossians 3:23

Discussion Questions

1. What does it mean to be faithful? (To keep doing something you said you would do. To keep your promises.)

2. What are some of the things you like to do or are good at doing? Encourage children to think beyond obvious talents such as reading well or playing sports to abilities such as being a good friend or listening well.

3. What are some ways to be faithful in using the abilities God has given you? (Practice using the abilities. Keep using them to help others. Have a good attitude while using the abilities.)

4. How can you use those abilities to serve God or help others? Answer this question with an example from your own life before asking children to respond.

Additional Information for Older Children

People were so amazed at Joni's story that they encouraged her to write a book about her life. Joni wrote an autobiography, and a movie was also made about her life. Now Joni has used her abilities to illustrate and write more books. (Optional: Bring a copy of her autobiography, *Joni*, to lend to an older child, or any of her children's books—*Tell Me the Truth, Tell Me the Promises, You've Got a Friend*—for children to borrow and read.)

Homes for the Homeless

Kindness is doing good without expecting anything in return.

Teacher's Materials
Bible with bookmark at 1 Thessalonians 3:12, hammer and/or other construction tools.

Introduce the Object Talk
When we do good without expecting anything in return, we are showing kindness. Let's look at a way some people work hard to show kindness even though they don't get paid any money for it.

Bible Verse

May the Lord make your love increase and overflow for each other and for everyone else, just as ours does for you.
1 Thessalonians 3:12

Present the Object Talk

1. Show hammer and/or other construction tools. **What do people use these tools for?** Volunteers tell ideas. **Carpenters who build furniture and houses usually get paid for their work. But some people who work as carpenters don't get paid at all! These people work for an organization called Habitat for Humanity. "Habitat" is a word that means the place where someone lives. "Humanity" is a word that means people. What do you think people who work for Habitat for Humanity might do?** (Build homes for people who don't have a good place to live.)

2. One man who works for Habitat for Humanity used to be the president of the United States. His name is Jimmy Carter. After a new president was elected, President Carter could have looked for a job to earn lots of money. But instead, because he loved God and wanted to show God's love to others, he decided to spend some of his time working for Habitat for Humanity.

Jimmy Carter and the other people who help Habitat for Humanity don't get any pay in return for building houses for poor people. They build houses because they want to show kindness to others in need.

Conclude

Read 1 Thessalonians 3:12 aloud. **How does this verse describe how we should show love? Something overflows when there's so much of it that it won't stay in one place. It spreads out everywhere! How does Jimmy Carter's kindness show God's love?** (He helps others without expecting to get money or anything else in return.) Pray, asking God to help your children find ways to be kind to others.

Bible Verse

May the Lord make your love increase and overflow for each other and for everyone else, just as ours does for you. 1 Thessalonians 3:12

Discussion Questions

1. What are some ways to show kindness to others without expecting anything in return? (Help a younger brother or sister. Donate items to a homeless shelter.)

2. When has someone been kind to you? What did that person do? Why do you think that person chose to be kind?

3. When have you been kind to another person? What happened as a result of your kindness?

Additional Information for Older Children

In 1981, the United States had a new president. Even though Jimmy Carter wasn't the president anymore, he and his wife, Rosalyn, still wanted to help people all over the world. They started the Carter Center, a nonprofit organization to help people be peaceful and treat others fairly. Through the years, the Carter Center has worked with many different countries to improve the way the people in those countries live. In 1999, Jimmy and Rosalyn Carter were presented with a very important award, the Presidential Medal of Freedom.

Eyes of Faith

Our right actions can help others do what is good.

Teacher's Materials

Bible with bookmark at 1 Timothy 4:12, one or more old eyeglasses or sunglasses with petroleum jelly smeared on the lenses.

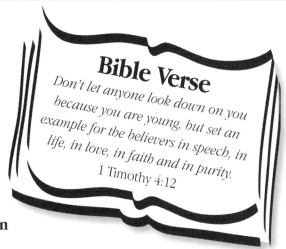

Bible Verse

Don't let anyone look down on you because you are young, but set an example for the believers in speech, in life, in love, in faith and in purity.

1 Timothy 4:12

Introduce the Object Talk

The good things we do and the right choices we make can help other people do good things, too. Let's find out how someone who couldn't see very well was an example to many people.

Present the Object Talk

1. Volunteers try on the glasses you prepared. **What are some things it would be hard to do if this is how you could see?** Children tell ideas. **A woman named Henrietta Mears had very poor eyesight, but that didn't stop her from doing great things.**

2. When Henrietta Mears was a child, her doctor said that she would probably become blind. So as she grew up, Henrietta decided to study hard, read a lot and memorize large portions of the Bible in case she later lost her eyesight. Henrietta's eyes were a problem for her throughout her life, but the doctor's prediction never did come true. She was never completely blind.

When Henrietta grew up, she became a high-school teacher in a small town. She was determined to help her students learn to do good things. When Henrietta discovered that her school didn't have a football team, she hired a coach and helped to organize the team. Henrietta went to every game to cheer for her students. Soon the football players started coming to Henrietta's Sunday School class where she taught them about the Bible. By the end of one year, many young people had decided to believe in Jesus and had learned to love and obey God because of Henrietta's teaching.

Conclude

Read 1 Timothy 4:12 aloud. **How was Henrietta Mears an example to others?** Children tell ideas. **Let's ask God to help us do what is right so that other people can learn about Him.** Lead children in prayer. **Jesus is the best example any of us can follow. Because of what Jesus did for us, we can become members of God's family.** Talk with interested children about becoming members of God's family (refer to "Leading a Child to Christ" article on p. 12).

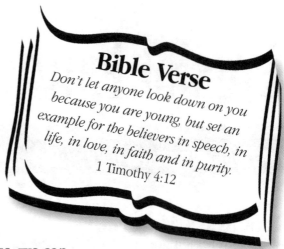

Bible Verse

Don't let anyone look down on you because you are young, but set an example for the believers in speech, in life, in love, in faith and in purity.
1 Timothy 4:12

Discussion Questions

1. Whose good example have you followed? Who might follow your good example? (Younger brother. Friend. Someone at school.) **How?**

2. What kinds of good actions might happen in a living room? In a kitchen? In a bedroom? (Helping a child with his or her homework. Clearing the dishes from the table. Reading a story to a younger brother or sister at bedtime. Sharing the computer.)

3. How might our right actions help another family member do good? (Reading a story to a younger brother might help him fall asleep. Clearing a table might help a parent have time to call a lonely friend.)

Additional Information for Older Children

Henrietta Mears was an example to many well-known Christian leaders, including Billy Graham. Henrietta started a publishing company that produces Sunday School curriculum. She also started a Christian camp that many children and adults attend every year. Her poor eyesight did not stop her from doing good!

The Lady with the Lamp

Generous and kind attitudes help us build friendships.

Teacher's Materials
Bible with bookmark at 1 Timothy 6:18, kerosene lantern or a flashlight.

Bible Verse
Command them to do good, to be rich in good deeds, and to be generous and willing to share. 1 Timothy 6:18

Introduce the Object Talk
We can build friendships by being generous and kind in our attitudes and actions. Let's find out what one lady did because she was so kind.

Present the Object Talk
1. Show lantern or flashlight. **When do people use lights like these? How might a light like this help when you are afraid in the dark?** Children respond. **In England during the 1800s, a woman named Florence Nightingale became known as "the Lady with the Lamp."**

2. When Florence Nightingale lived, hospitals were nothing like they are now. There were very few doctors and nurses, and people didn't understand that germs make people sick. Hospitals weren't kept very clean. Many people who went to hospitals became sicker instead of getting better.

When Florence became a nurse, she believed God wanted her to change things! She used her own money to buy clean clothes for patients. She hired people to wash sheets and blankets. Florence often worked until late at night, carrying a lamp through the hospital as she checked on her patients. She was never too tired to help someone.

As Florence worked, she also talked to people about Jesus. Florence—"the Lady with the Lamp"—helped people learn about Jesus' love and saved the lives of many sick or injured people because of her kindness and generosity.

Conclude

Read 1 Timothy 6:18 aloud. **How was Florence Nightingale kind and willing to share? What does it mean to have a generous attitude?** Children tell ideas. **Let's ask God to help us build friendships by being generous and kind this week.** Lead children in prayer.

Bible Verse
Command them to do good, to be rich in good deeds, and to be generous and willing to share. 1 Timothy 6:18

Discussion Questions

1. **What are some generous or kind actions kids your age can do? How might these actions help to build friendships?**

2. Read 1 Timothy 6:18. **How can we "be rich in good deeds"?** (Do good things often.)

3. **How would obeying 1 Timothy 6:18 help the kids in your school?**

Additional Information for Older Children

Because of the help Florence Nightingale gave soldiers during the war, she became a national hero in England. The Nightingale School of Nursing in London was started to honor her kind actions. In addition to the many honors and awards Florence received, she was the first woman to receive the British Order of Merit, a very important award.

Double Trouble

We can show God's love through attitudes and words that are gentle and respectful.

Teacher's Materials

Bible with bookmark at 2 Timothy 2:24,25; photograph of a newborn or young baby.

Introduce the Object Talk

Our gentle and respectful words and attitudes show God's love to others. Let's find out about a woman who was gentle and respectful, even though she didn't agree with what others were doing.

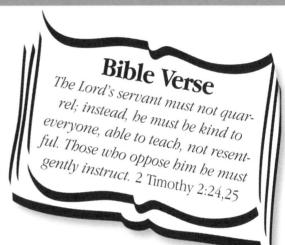

Bible Verse

The Lord's servant must not quarrel; instead, he must be kind to everyone, able to teach, not resentful. Those who oppose him he must gently instruct. 2 Timothy 2:24,25

Present the Object Talk

1. Show photograph of baby. **How do people usually treat a newborn or young baby?** Children respond. **Many years ago, people in a village in Africa felt afraid when they saw babies who were twins. These people believed that twin babies were evil and should be killed. The people wouldn't even walk on a road on which a mother of twins had walked!**

2. In 1876, a woman named Mary Slessor lived near this village. Mary wanted to help the people there learn about God's love. One day, Mary heard that twins had been born in the village. Mary quickly

ran through the jungle to the village, hoping to save the lives of the babies. When Mary arrived, one of the babies was already dead, but the other one was alive. Mary gently took the baby and started walking back with the baby's mother to Mary's house.

As she was walking on the road, however, Mary realized that if the mother walked on the road, the people wouldn't walk on that road again. They would have to work hard to cut a new road through the jungle. So instead of ignoring the people's beliefs, Mary respected them and had a path cut through the jungle straight to her house. Mary took care of the baby, and soon many people in the village learned to love the baby, too. And best of all, because of Mary's gentle actions, the people kept coming to her house and learned about God's love for them!

Bible Verse

The Lord's servant must not quarrel; instead, he must be kind to everyone, able to teach, not resentful. Those who oppose him he must gently instruct. 2 Timothy 2:24,25

Conclude

Read 2 Timothy 2:24,25 aloud. **People who love God are sometimes called servants. How did Mary Slessor show that she was God's servant?** (She was gentle and kind and helped others learn about Jesus.) **Let's ask God to help us remember to use words and attitudes that are gentle and respectful.** Lead children in prayer.

Discussion Questions

1. When has someone treated you gently and respectfully? What did they do? What did you do?

2. Why do you think God wants us to treat others gently and respectfully? (Because He loves all people.)

3. What are some gentle and kind words you like to hear? ("Thank you." "Sorry." "You can have the first turn." Words that are encouraging instead of bossy. Words that show we care about the other person.) **When is it hard to use kind and gentle words?**

Additional Information for Older Children

One time when Mary Slessor needed to build a new building to use in teaching people in the village about God, she asked the chief of the village for help. Though the chief agreed to send people to help her, several days passed and no one showed up. Instead of yelling and complaining, Mary simply started doing the work herself! Mary chose to be gentle and kind, even when it was hard.

Talk Radio

Teacher's Materials

Bible with bookmark at James 1:19, one or more copies of Chronicles of Narnia books (available in most church and public libraries).

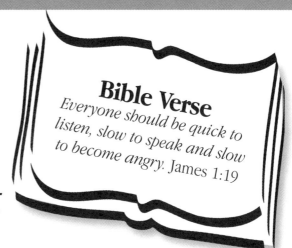

Bible Verse

Everyone should be quick to listen, slow to speak and slow to become angry. James 1:19

Introduce the Object Talk

One way to show self-control is to be careful about what you say. Let's find out how one man was careful about what he said.

Present the Object Talk

1. Show book(s) you brought. **The Chronicles of Narnia is a series of books written by a man named C. S. Lewis. What do you know about these books?** Volunteers tell about stories they know. **C. S. Lewis wrote these books to help children learn about loving and obeying God. But Mr. Lewis also did many other things in his life.**

The Lion, the Witch and the Wardrobe by C.S. Lewis

2. Clive Staples Lewis was born in Ireland in 1898. He joined the army to fight for England during World War I and was a brave army officer. But during World War II, C. S. Lewis helped people in another way in England.

During the war, while the Nazis were bombing cities in England, many people listened to C. S. Lewis talk on the radio about what it meant to be a Christian. C. S. Lewis carefully chose what to say so that all kinds of people could understand God's love for them, even when bad things, like a war, happened. The talks helped people see that loving and obeying God was the most important thing to do. So many people were helped by the radio talks that later some of the talks were written down in a book called *Mere Christianity*. Even today people learn about being part of God's family from this book.

Conclude

Read James 1:19 aloud. **Being "slow to speak" means being careful about what you say. How did C. S. Lewis show that he was careful in the things he said?** (When talking on the radio, he was careful about what he said so that all kinds of people could learn about God.) **When we listen to others and are careful about what we say, we show self-control. Let's ask God to help us listen to each other and use self-control in what we say.** Lead children in prayer.

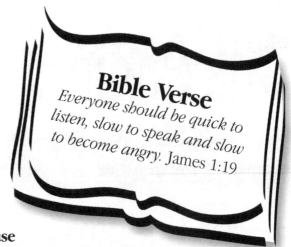

Bible Verse
Everyone should be quick to listen, slow to speak and slow to become angry. James 1:19

Discussion Questions

1. When might it be hard to show self-control when you talk to others? (When angry or upset. When someone says something unkind.)

2. When are some times it might be difficult for kids your age to listen? (When they're tired. When they're hungry. When someone is taking a long time to speak.)

3. What can you do that will help you listen better and control what you say? (Follow James 1:19 and be "quick to listen" and "slow to speak." Pray and ask God for His help. Count to 10 before speaking if upset. Walk away before saying something that shouldn't be said.)

4. What should we do when we make mistakes and say things we shouldn't? (Ask for God's forgiveness and apologize to the people we were talking to.)

Additional Information for Older Children

Many people wrote letters to C. S. Lewis, and he spent a lot of time answering the letters, many of them from children who read the Chronicles of Narnia. Some of the letters he wrote back to these children were published in a book called *Letters to Children.* Invite children to tell what they would write in letters to C. S. Lewis. (Optional: Read aloud some of the letters from *Letters to Children* by C. S. Lewis.)

Peace in the Congo

Because God has forgiven us through Christ, encourage people to forgive each other and make peace.

Teacher's Materials
Bible with bookmark at 1 Peter 3:8, world map.

Introduce the Object Talk
We can encourage people to forgive each other and make peace, because God has forgiven us. Let's find out about one man who worked hard to help people and make peace.

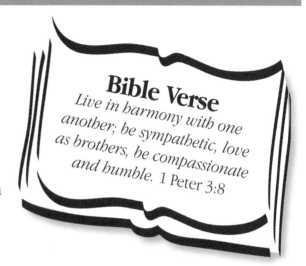

Bible Verse
Live in harmony with one another; be sympathetic, love as brothers, be compassionate and humble. 1 Peter 3:8

Present the Object Talk

1. Show children the map. **Where is the country in which we live?** Volunteer locates country on map. Show children or ask an older child to find the country of the Democratic Republic of the Congo (formerly Zaire). **William Sheppard was an African-American missionary to the Congo in 1890. He went to this country because many of the tribes of people who lived there did not know about Jesus.**

2. William learned the different languages the people in the Congo spoke and helped the people build churches, schools and homes for children. William even became friends with a tribe of people who had always killed any outsiders who came to their area. William's work with these people made him so famous that he was invited three times to the White House, home of the president of the United States.

William could have felt like he had done enough to help the people in the Congo, but he knew that there was a lot more important work left to do. At that time, the king of Belgium was in control of the Congo. His soldiers forced many people in the Congo to work under terrible conditions. William began to write about the problems he saw. Soon people all around the world learned about these problems and convinced the king of Belgium to treat the people in the Congo in better ways.

Conclude

Read 1 Peter 3:8 aloud. **Which instructions in this verse tell ways to make peace?** ("Live in harmony with one another." "Be sympathetic.") **How did William Sheppard obey this verse? How can you make peace with others? Let's ask God to help us encourage people to forgive each other and make peace.** Lead children in prayer. **Making peace with others is a good way to show that we love God and are members of His family.** Talk with interested children about becoming members of God's family (refer to "Leading a Child to Christ" article on p. 12).

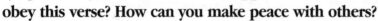

Bible Verse

Live in harmony with one another; be sympathetic, love as brothers, be compassionate and humble. 1 Peter 3:8

Discussion Questions

1. People can "live in harmony" with each other when they choose to respect each other. What can you do to show more respect and kindness to your friends? Your family?

2. How do you think living in harmony, or respecting each other, can make peace?

3. Forgiving others is one way to "live in harmony" with others. What can a kid your age do when it seems difficult to forgive others? (Ask for God's help. Read about God's forgiveness in the Bible. Forgive, even when it's hard.)

Additional Information for Older Children

William Sheppard's wife, Lucy Gantt Sheppard, traveled with her husband to the Congo. She worked hard to help the people in the Congo have a good education. Lucy wrote books in the language of the people who lived in the Congo. She wrote the very first reading book written in their language.

Traveling School

Goodness includes using what God gives you to help others.

Teacher's Materials
Bible with bookmark at 1 Peter 4:10, peanuts.

Introduce the Object Talk
Using what God gives us to help others is a big part of showing goodness. Let's find out how one man used what God had given him to help others.

Bible Verse
Each one should use whatever gift he has received to serve others. 1 Peter 4:10

Present the Object Talk
1. Show peanuts. **What are some things that people use peanuts for?** (To eat. To make peanut butter.) **Before the early 1900s, few people grew peanuts because they didn't know how to use the peanuts. But a man named George Washington Carver believed that God had given him a brain to help him discover how the peanut could be used. Dr. Carver discovered over 300 things that could be made from peanuts, including printer's ink, a milk substitute, face powder, soap and candy.** (Note: If child indicates he or she is allergic to peanuts, comment, **While some people are allergic to peanuts, there are other good uses for them besides eating them.**)

2. Dr. Carver also discovered many things about the best ways to grow plants. And he didn't keep what he learned to himself! Dr. Carver used what he had learned about plants to help others.

Dr. Carver and a friend got a horse and wagon and set up a portable school. They traveled to poor farms all over their county to teach African-American farmers better ways to grow plants. He also taught them new ways to use the things they grew so that they could make money selling new products. Some people complained that Dr. Carver should make people pay to learn the things he was teaching. But

Dr. Carver insisted that money was not important. Dr. Carver told people that it didn't matter how much money they had or how fancy their clothes were. He said that serving others was more important than money or clothes. In fact, in one of his jobs, Dr. Carver didn't accept a pay raise for 40 years! All that mattered to him was helping people.

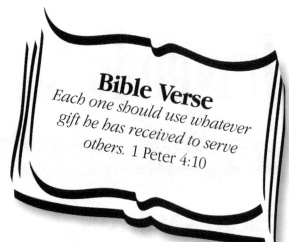

Bible Verse
Each one should use whatever gift he has received to serve others. 1 Peter 4:10

Conclude
Read 1 Peter 4:10 aloud. **How did George Washington Carver show goodness and obey 1 Peter 4:10?** Lead children in prayer, asking God to help them find good ways to help others.

Discussion Questions
1. Who is someone you know that shows goodness? What does he or she do?

2. What are some things you enjoy doing or are good at doing? How can you use these things to help others?

3. Who are some people you can help or serve this week?

Additional Information for Older Children
When Dr. Carver first began teaching people how to grow better crops, some of the farmers didn't believe what he said. So as part of his teaching, Dr. Carver would show them sample plants and patiently explain how to grow the plants. Sometimes Dr. Carver would even cook a good-tasting meal to show people how they could make food from their crops. (Optional: Volunteers taste chickpeas (garbanzo beans), one of the foods Dr. Carver taught others to eat.)

Jungle Fever

Teacher's Materials

Bible with bookmark at 1 John 3:16, jungle item (fern, picture of jungle animals from a nature magazine, tape of jungle sounds, rainstick or other artifact, video of jungle scenery, etc.).

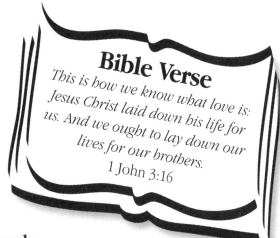

Bible Verse

This is how we know what love is: Jesus Christ laid down his life for us. And we ought to lay down our lives for our brothers.
1 John 3:16

Introduce the Object Talk

Jesus' words and actions when He lived on Earth showed us what love is like. Let's find out how some people who lived in a jungle learned about Jesus' life and His love for them.

Present the Object Talk

1. Show and describe the jungle item you brought. **What would you like about living in a jungle? What do you think might be difficult about living there?** Children respond. **One tribe of people who lived in a jungle in New Guinea had a difficult time, because they often fought with another tribe. New Guinea is near Australia.**

2. A man named Don Richardson, his wife and their little boy went to live in New Guinea and teach these tribes about Jesus. Don learned that one tradition the tribes had for making peace was to give one of their own babies to the tribe with whom they were fighting. That baby was called a peace child. As long as that baby was kept alive and well, the tribes would stay at peace with each other. But if anything happened to the baby, the tribes would be at war again.

Don told the people about Jesus by describing Jesus as God's peace child. He told them that God gave Jesus to all people to make peace between God and people

forever. After hearing Don's words, the people understood what God's love is like and that Jesus made it possible for sin to be forgiven and for people to live in peace with each other. The people in the village never had to give one of their own children as a peace child again.

Bible Verse

This is how we know what love is: Jesus Christ laid down his life for us. And we ought to lay down our lives for our brothers.

1 John 3:16

Conclude

Read 1 John 3:16 aloud. **How would you describe Jesus' love for us?** Children respond. **What is a way Don Richardson showed that he loved Jesus?** (He helped other people learn about Jesus.) Lead children in prayer, thanking God for Jesus and for His love for them.

Discussion Questions

1. What are some ways Jesus showed love to people? (Cared for people's needs. Helped them get well. Gave them food. Was kind to them. Taught them.)

2. What is one way to show love like Jesus did when you are at school? In your neighborhood? (Forgive someone when he or she says something rude or mean. Invite kids whom other people usually ignore to play a game.)

3. What might happen if we were to show love in some of the ways that Jesus showed love?

4. What are some ways we can show God's love to others? (Be kind to younger kids. Help people who are hungry or sick. Tell others about Jesus and how to become members of God's family. Be kind and show love to brothers and sisters.)

Additional Information for Older Children

Don Richardson has written several books. One of his books, *Peace Child*, tells about the Sawi people and how their lives changed as a result of learning about Jesus. *Eternity in Their Hearts* has many short stories about groups of people from around the world and how they learned about Jesus. (Optional: Bring to class one or more of Don Richardson's books and invite interested children to borrow books for the week.)

Worldwide Travel

Teacher's Materials

Bible with bookmark at 1 John 3:18, world map.

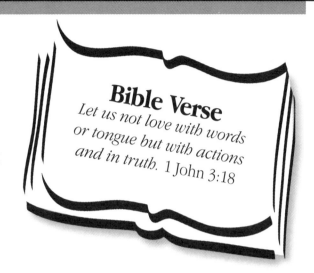

Bible Verse
Let us not love with words or tongue but with actions and in truth. 1 John 3:18

Introduce the Object Talk

We can show God's goodness by making sure that our words and actions match. Let's find out about a man who became known for loving and obeying God with both his words and actions.

Present the Object Talk

1. Show world map. Invite a volunteer to point out the country in which you live. **What other countries have you traveled to or heard of?** Volunteers name countries. Invite volunteers to locate countries on map. Give help as needed. **Today we are going to talk about a man named Billy Graham. He has traveled to over 185 countries!**

2. In 1934, Billy Graham went to a church meeting and heard a preacher talk about Jesus. Because of what he learned about Jesus at that meeting, Billy decided to love and serve God for his whole life. So after Billy went to college, he started telling people about Jesus' love and how to become a member of God's family.

Billy not only told people about Jesus' love, but his actions also showed Jesus' love. Billy traveled to cities all over the world to preach about Jesus. He talked to people who were kings and to people who were members of tribes in Africa. He preached in huge football stadiums and in small villages. Every place that Billy preached, many people decided to become members of God's family. Everyone that met Billy saw that both his actions and words showed Jesus' love.

Conclude

Read 1 John 3:18 aloud. **Billy Graham's words and actions showed that he obeyed this verse. Who are some other people you know who love God and others with their actions as well as with their words?** Volunteers briefly tell about people they know. **Let's ask God to help us show goodness by making sure our words and actions match.** Lead children in prayer. **Billy Graham used his words to help other people become members of God's family.** Talk with interested children about becoming members of God's family (refer to "Leading a Child to Christ" article on p. 12).

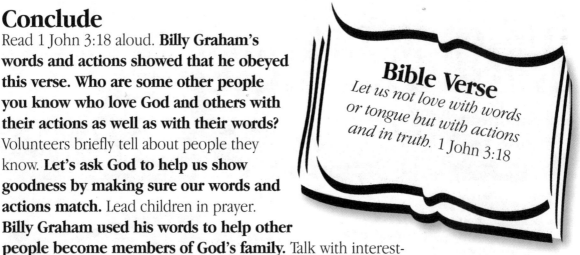

Bible Verse
Let us not love with words or tongue but with actions and in truth. 1 John 3:18

Discussion Questions

1. Why is it important for what you do to match what you say you believe? (Our actions show what we really believe. Our good actions can help others do what is good.)

2. When are some times it might be hard for a kid your age to act in ways that show goodness? How could you help a friend in a situation like this?

3. Making our words match our actions is one way to show goodness. How does God help us have the fruit of goodness? (Gives the Bible to help us understand right ways to act. Reminds us of ways to speak and act to show goodness. Answers our prayers for help.)

Additional Information for Older Children

Billy Graham's son, Franklin Graham, also traveled and preached about God. Franklin Graham also became the leader of Samaritan's Purse, a group of people who help people all over the world. For many years at Christmastime, Samaritan's Purse has collected shoe boxes of gifts that are given to poor children in many countries. (Optional: Find additional information at www.samaritanspurse.org.)

Index

Biographical Index

Fruit of the Spirit Index

The fruit of the Spirit is love, joy, peace, patience, kindness,
goodness, faithfulness, gentleness and self-control.
Against such things there is no law. Galatians 5:22,23

Fruit of the Spirit

Love

Joy

Peace

Patience

Kindness

Goodness

Faithfulness

Gentleness

Self-Control

Gospel Light is God's Word for a Kid's World!

Sunday School Curriculum

What do kids need most today? To know Jesus and have a safe place where they can grow. Gospel Light Sunday School curriculum makes it easy for you to provide that place in your church. From our *Little Blessings Nursery Kit* to *Planet 56* for fifth and sixth grades, Gospel Light provides everything you need: teacher-friendly teacher's guides, colorful and fun student pages, engaging activities, great music and more.

Vacation Bible School

Gospel Light is the creative and fun choice for churches that love to reach children for Jesus. Each summer, we provide a highly evangelistic program that makes it easy for you to create an incredible environment at your church—where children will want to come to experience great Bible stories, skits, crafts, games and songs. It will be the highlight of your children's ministry year!

For every age, and at every time, Gospel Light's flexible programs help you bring God's Word to a kid's world. Try them for yourself and see! For **FREE curriculum samples**, to order a starter kit, or to receive more information, please call your curriculum supplier or **1-800-4-GOSPEL**.

Gospel Light

Big Bible Learning Fun!

The Big Book of Kindergarten Puzzles
A full year's worth of fun Bible puzzles—mazes, dot-to-dots, letters, shapes and more! Bible story and verse puzzles to go with every lesson! Reproducible.
Manual • 216p
ISBN 08307.27574

The Big Book of Instant Activities
Over 100 fun, simple activities to help teachers with transitions, regaining attention and just having fun! Reproducible.
Manual • 176p
ISBN 08307.26624

The Big Book of Christian Growth
Discipling made easy! 306 discussion cards based on Bible passages, and 75 games and activities for preteens. Reproducible.
Manual •176p
ISBN 08307.25865

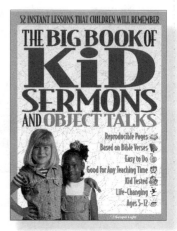

The Big Book of Kid Sermons and Object Talks
Relate Bible principles to young lives with object talks. Ages 5 to 12.
Manual •112p
ISBN 08307.25164

The Big Book of Service Projects
Over 80 reproducible service projects. Many can be completed in class!
Manual •176p
ISBN 08307.26330

Read-Aloud Story and Activity Book, Vol. 1
Reproducible coloring activities and contemporary stories about Bible truths.
Complete instructions and questions on every page.
Manual • 222p
ISBN 08307.27701

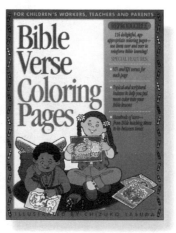

Bible Verse Coloring Pages
Bible learning with crayons. Includes 116 verses in both *NIV* and *KJV* translations. Reproducible.
Manual • 240p
SPCN 25116.06720

Bible Verse Coloring Pages #2
Reproducible coloring pictures for children ages 5 to 8. Includes both *NIV* and *KJV* verses.
Manual • 216p
ISBN 08307.25857

Available from your Gospel Light supplier or call **1-800-4-GOSPEL.**

Gospel Light
God's Word for a Kid's World!

Smart Resources for Your Children's Ministry

Sunday School Smart Pages
Edited by Wes and Sheryl Haystead
Training, inspiration, materials, quick solutions and more for teaching ages 2 through 12.
Reproducible.
Manual • ISBN 08307.15215

Sunday School Promo Pages
Wes and Sheryl Haystead
Resources and advice to recruit teachers, gain church support, increase attendance and more.
Reproducible.
Manual • ISBN 08307.15894

5th & 6th Grade Smart Pages
Wes Haystead and Tom Prinz
The most current information, tips and quick solutions for teaching 5th and 6th grades, plus parent education articles.
Reproducible.
Manual • ISBN 08307.18052

Nursery Smart Pages
Legal and safety guidelines, teacher's pages, parent pages, classroom activities, clip art, and much more!
Reproducible.
Manual • ISBN 08307.19067

VBS Smart Pages
Advice, answers and articles for a successful Vacation Bible School. Includes forms, records and clip art.
Reproducible.
Manual • ISBN 08307.16718

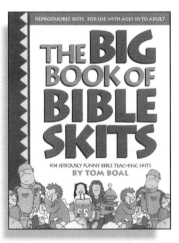

The Big Book of Bible Skits
Tom Boal
104 seriously funny Bible teaching skits. Includes discussion questions.
Reproducible.
Manual • ISBN 08307.19164

The Big Book of Theme Parties, Snacks & Games
Decorating ideas, snack recipes, wacky activities, games, clip art, and more for eight complete themes.
Reproducible.
Manual • ISBN 08307.18206

The Big Book of Bible Games
200 fun games that teach Bible concepts and life application.
Reproducible.
ISBN 08307.18214

Available from your Gospel Light supplier or call **1-800-4-GOSPEL**.